CORAL S[EA]

Cairns

Townsville

BOWEN

STANBROKE

LDERLEY

BANCHORY ○

Rockhampton
Gladstone

QUEENSLAND

⊖ TANBAR

Quilpie

Cunnamulla

Toowoomba

BRISBANE

NEW SOUTH
WALES

Bourke

Dubbo

Sydney

VICTORIA

Canberra

*

BORTHWICK-OWNED WORKS AT TOWNS SHOWN THUS: ■
BORTHWICK-OWNED CATTLE STATIONS --------- ○
ROCKLANDS STATION PTY. LTD. IN WHICH --------- ⊖
BORTHWICKS HAVE A SHARE HOLDING

	over 120
	80 –120
ANNUAL RAINFALL in inches	40 – 80
	20 – 40
	under 20

TASMAN SEA

MELBOURNE

Launceston

TASMANIA

Hobart

87.50

BORTHWICKS *A Century in the Meat Trade* 1863–1963

There is no work on the world's carpet greater than this in which
I have been engaged. . . . The time . . . is not far distant, when
the various portions of the earth will give forth their products for
the use of each and all. . . . 'The Earth is the Lord's and the fulness
thereof', and it is certainly within the compass of man to ensure
that all His people shall be partakers of that fulness.

THOMAS MORT,
pioneer of refrigerated meat shipment,
who died at Bodalla, New South Wales,
in 1878

SIR THOMAS BORTHWICK, BART, THE FOUNDER. 1835-1912

BORTHWICKS

A Century in the Meat Trade, 1863-1963

BY GODFREY HARRISON

DRAWINGS BY DONALD BURFIELD MILLS AND MAPS BY LEO VERNON

LONDON · 1963

Designed, printed and bound in England by Hazell Watson & Viney Limited, Aylesbury, Bucks

Contents

Some readers will be interested to know what a freezing works originally cost, what its value is today and the number of stock it kills. Probably many more will not; in their interests most statistical data of this nature are collected at the end of the chapter in which the works is first mentioned.

Illustrations

Acknowledgments

Acknowledgments are made to the following for photographs reproduced on the pages mentioned. The Australian Geographical Society, page 56; The Australian National Travel Association, page 176 (two); Central Office of Information, page 79; National Publicity Studio, Wellington, New Zealand, pages 113, 116, 117, 119, 120, 169; Peter Newbolt, pages 76, 77; Queensland Country Life, page 172 (top). In addition special thanks are due to Mr Michael Ayrton for kind permission to reproduce the pencil drawing of Mr A. M. Borthwick, the present Chairman, on page 51. The drawing of the Whitburgh coat of arms, reproduced on page 84, is by Mr Leo Vernon.

Introduction

The story of every successful firm is worth reading, if only because we all want to know how it was done.

The answer always contains certain common elements—a need and an opportunity, clear enough to all today, perhaps, but seen at the time by one man or by a chosen few; a struggle of human vision and character against unforeseeable obstacles; a contribution to the world's well-being. But in its working out each story is startlingly different. Not only the aims and the circumstances but the characters are different. One feels that often the people concerned, by doing what another man would not have done, have each, to a greater or less degree, imparted their own direction to events. So they become part of history. This is exciting. It is an antidote to the rather depressing idea—too easy to accept in these scientific days—that we are all units in some vast equation, determined by causes beyond our understanding or control. Man the individual stands for something after all.

This particular story is concerned with a staple food—meat. It is concerned with events which have revolutionised the food supply of industrial countries that cannot grow all they eat, and have brought prosperity to others that at one time could not dispose of their surplus. Geographically, it covers the widest field possible. It links the butcher's shop in Britain with the wide open spaces of the Commonwealth. It combines developments of great economic importance with true stories of drought, flood, fire and earthquake. In time, it covers a century that saw unparalleled growth in the great Dominions and, in Britain, a transformation of ideas from the clear, confident, limited philosophy of Victorian days to a much wider, if less easily defined, conception of business obligations and relationships.

And here the author would like to pay a tribute. A work of this kind is usually deprived of its sting through a desire to avoid saying anything, particularly in print, that could possibly lead to controversy or provoke a retort. The Borthwick directors have been remarkably free from these inhibitions. They have opened their minds on such matters as their own motives and those of their ancestors; certain decisions which they now consider to have been mistaken; the effects—sometimes in their opinion for the worse— of actions by Governments; and the part played in commercial decisions by the shadow of the tax inspector. The results are enlightening.

Variety is the spice of life, but a story must hold together. This story is held together by the fact that it records the doings of one family and one family firm, though against a background of world-wide needs and world-wide developments. It is held together by the name of Borthwick. It is unusual in these days to find a firm which, after a hundred years of remarkable growth and ramification, remains so largely under the control of its founder's direct descendants. But there are many other families also, in Britain and on the other side of the world, who have been faithful to the same firm from generation to generation. Individuals too, thousands of them, who, in spite of their differences of character and the different jobs they do, have become parts of a single whole; so that Borthwicks has come to stand for something distinctive to all who come in contact with it. These people *are* the firm. This is their story.

It is their story although very few of their names appear in it. It would obviously be impossible to bring them all in. And those that do come in are here, not necessarily because they merit it more than many others, but because they take part in some incident, or illustrate some point, which seemed to demand a place. There has been no other method in the author's madness so far as the choice of names is concerned. This is the only sort of apology he can offer to many good men—young or old, living or dead—whom he has got to know face to face or by repute, and has learned to admire and respect.

There be of them that have left a name behind them,
That their praises might be reported.
And some there be which have no memorial . . .

Ecclesiasticus, 44, 8–9

Thomas Borthwick

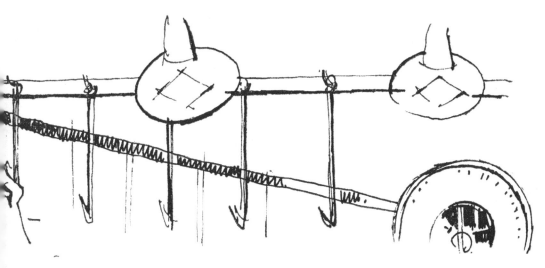

CHAPTER ONE

Foundations

Early in the nineteenth century two brothers, Thomas and Alexander Borthwick, owned a butcher's shop at Ratho, on the outskirts of Edinburgh. It was evidently a prosperous business and earned respect, for later in life Thomas was made a freeman of Edinburgh; and his great-grandson, now chairman of Thomas Borthwick & Sons, has in his possession a snuff-box with this inscription:

Presented To

Mr Alexr. Borthwick

BY A FEW OF THE CATTLE AGENTS & BUTCHERS

of Edinburgh

AS A TOKEN OF RESPECT & ESTEEM

June 13th, 1865

However, these two claim a place in this story chiefly through a child—son of Thomas and nephew of Alexander—who was born at Musselburgh on the 11th January 1835, was christened Thomas after his father, and in due time founded the firm which bears his name today.

Of young Thomas's upbringing little is known beyond the fact that his family were solid, respectable, early Victorian folk, and staunch members of the Scottish Presbyterian church. These influences will be apparent when we come to describe the character and views of the man. One caution: we must not be over-impressed by ideas of grim severity. Discipline was certainly the vogue; but those times were no less notable for immense vitality, and for the kind of happiness that radiates around parents who are as loving as they are dutiful. Some of us today, alas, have nearly forgotten what the word 'family' meant a hundred and more years ago. But without it, it is impossible to understand the story of almost any firm in Britain that was founded about that time and has grown and flourished ever since.

Naturally the boy was soon lending a hand in the business. Amongst the houses to which he delivered joints of meat was a distinguished one, Lord Rosebery's, wherein in later life he was a guest—a change of fortune which is much commoner now than it was then. But it was soon apparent that his real flair lay in livestock dealing. Butchers were much involved in this business in those times—as indeed they are today in country districts. Young Thomas Borthwick had a good eye for a beast. Like any good livestock buyer, he could walk among a flock of a thousand sheep and tell the weight and value of any one of them at a glance. Perhaps he was better than most, for in time he became a judge at the 'Royal'.

When he had some experience and perhaps a little money he left home and started business on his own in 1863, which becomes the starting point of this history. He is recorded principally as a livestock agent at Liverpool and Manchester in the early days. The story is told that sometimes when he was dissatisfied with prices offered for stock, he bought some and had it slaughtered on his own account and sold the meat. So he developed from agent to principal. The year 1863 was a bad time for Lancashire and one might ask why he chose to set up there. The American Civil war was in its third year, the cotton imports to the United Kingdom had fallen disastrously and over a quarter of a million people were unemployed in the Lancashire cotton industry. This recession may have triggered off in his mind the possibility of importing meat cheaper than it could be produced in England.

As to his reasons for the move—he had already a fairly large connection round Carlisle and it may be that, with the growth of the railways and the increasing industrialisation of Merseyside and the Lancashire cotton towns about that time, Manchester offered better outlets for surplus stock from the Border than did Edinburgh. On the other hand there is a family tradition that he was attracted by the imports of cattle 'on the hoof' from the United States and Canada which had then just started coming into Liverpool. There is much to be said for this theory. He is known to have been greatly impressed with the malnutrition prevalent among the crowded masses in the big towns, and to have held the view that it could and should be remedied. He may well have already conceived the ambition to do what he could, within his own province, towards that end. It must have been evident that, with a growing population in a very small island, the only solution was to import; and at that time the only way to import fresh meat was on the hoof.

Apparently he prospered; for in 1870 he took a twenty-one-year lease of a farm in North Wales. There is no reason to think that the farm was intended to have any connection with the business, nor to make any contribution to income—perhaps rather the reverse. Thomas had a natural love of farming for its own sake.

Also perhaps he was thinking of his coming marriage, which took place the following January. His wife was Letitia Banks, of Liverpool. Her family also were active in the meat trade. The firm of Richard Banks & Sons, shipping butchers, was founded in 1793 and is still going strong. But Thomas can have had no idea then what a vital part the marriage connection was to play in the future of his business.

The Franco-Prussian war was over. The usual slump followed; and Thomas Borthwick felt the draught. He now had a wife, and no doubt the couple were looking forward to the large family with which in time they were blessed. He also had a farm that, at the rent to which he was committed, could not possibly pay its way. It is characteristic of the man that he met this situation, not by retrenchment, but by expanding his business. In the year of his marriage—1871—he began to sell in the Liverpool market as well as in Manchester.

This development was a success. Three years later Thomas bought a house in Liverpool, which for twenty years was to share with the Welsh farm the function of family home.

Elm House was excellent for the purpose: a large, solid, comfortable, Victorian house standing in the Old Swan district, well out in the country, though near enough to the market for Thomas to walk across the fields to his daily labours. It is still there, though surrounded by other houses and offices. Now called Elms House, it is a youth employment bureau. Lorries and cars roar past through what must once have been its garden. *Sic transit* . . .

Before long the home rang with the cries of children. It was a typical Victorian family. First came a daughter, Eleanor; then, in 1874, the son and heir—Thomas, of course, with the addition of his mother's maiden name,

Banks; James Alexander in 1876; Letitia Mary in 1878; William in 1879; Algernon in 1881; and finally, after a lapse of six years, there was another daughter, Sybil.

From them, direct or through their own children, come memories that help to build a picture of the family life (not irrelevant, for here future Borthwicks are being made). One shows young Tom at the farm in North Wales, the night before the harvesters are due, going to bed in his boots so as to be ready for work early in the morning. Another is of Sundays, again at the farm, when whistling was banned, and the evenings were spent in games of mental arithmetic around the fire.

Parental discipline was evidently strict, but not more so than was normal among respectable people at the time; and it certainly did not inhibit the children's vitality and (a word that we find turning up time and again in letters written about early days by Thomas Banks Borthwick fifty or sixty years later) keenness.

Father Thomas was a lifelong abstainer, and always refused to invest in brewery shares; but he was not fanatical on the subject. He did not seek to apply his rules rigidly to others except when he felt that efficiency in work was affected. He was adamant in his belief that liquor was bad for mental alertness—in which he has the support of scientific tests. And we must not forget what a raging curse alcohol was eighty and more years ago. Much the same applies to his views on betting. All his life he was a sincere supporter of the Presbyterian church, which he served as sidesman and elder. In politics he was a convinced radical, an adherent of Gladstone rather than of Lloyd George.

That his strictness was tempered with humanity one story will suffice to show. It was told thirty years ago by a retired employee who was then between eighty-five and ninety years of age. At the time in question this man was a salesman on the Manchester market. He was a heavy drinker and was often drunk at work. Thomas Borthwick offered him an extra half-crown a week—a big sum in those days—if he would stop drinking. The man agreed and received the increase. Not long afterwards the master found him drunk in the market again and dismissed him. The following week he was there working as usual. 'What are you doing here? I dismissed you.' The man answered: 'Who am I to work for if I don't work for you?' He continued to work for Borthwicks until he retired in the fullness of years.

By 1880 Thomas Borthwick had built up a sound business, with depots in Manchester and Liverpool; to which two more, in Glasgow and Birmingham, were added within a few years. He had his farm in Wales, his comfortable house in the suburbs of Liverpool, and a growing family. All seems set for a life of steady if uneventful progress. But meanwhile something was happening on the other side of the world which was to change the whole story.

Schooner Strathleven. Launched 1875; iron hull; engine 220 h.p.

CHAPTER TWO

Revolution in the Meat Trade

The problem of meat shortage and malnutrition in Britain—and to some degree in all industrial countries—was getting steadily worse as the urban masses multiplied. The problem in Australia, New Zealand and other pastoral countries was equal and opposite. Large flocks roamed over huge tracts of land, unfenced and tended by lonely shepherds. Sheep were valued for their wool, not for their meat (except what could be consumed locally); and cattle were often worth little more than their hides. New Zealand had thirty-eight sheep for every man, woman and child in the country, and surplus animals sold for a shilling or sixpence a head in 1871. In Australia, when the price of wool slumped, millions of sheep went to the boiling-down works around Sydney in a single year: the price they fetched was the value of the tallow that could be extracted from the carcase; because this was exportable. Meanwhile countless square miles in the outback, potentially the finest cattle country, were possessed by the bush turkey and the kangaroo.

A cannery had been started in New South Wales as long ago as 1847, and by 1880 Britain was importing some 16 million pounds of canned meat from the United States, South America, Australia and New Zealand. But this was no substitute for fresh meat, and the quantity was hardly enough to make any difference. The country could easily have absorbed that number of whole carcases. (And in fact this is less than the quantity of sheep and lambs that New Zealand alone sends to Britain annually today, as noted later in this chapter.) Some live cattle were coming to Liverpool from North America—an expensive business involving the risk of casualties; and the length of the voyage put the more distant dominions out of competition.

A number of men had their minds on the problem of how to keep meat in good condition while transporting it half-way round the world; and they realised that the answer was refrigeration. Among them was Thomas Mort, a self-made man and pioneer of several developments in Australia. Impressed by a story which he read in his newspaper of a prehistoric monster that had been found perfectly preserved in a mass of ice, he set an engineer to work on methods of freezing or chilling meat, and in 1861 started the first freezing works in the world at Darling Harbour, near Sydney. With financial support from the Sydney Chamber of Commerce and Australian squatters a sailing ship was chartered, fitted with ammonia freezing apparatus similar to that used on land, and laden with a cargo of frozen meat for England.

The apparatus was nearly right but not quite. There was a risk that the pipes carrying brine, strained by the ship's movement, would leak. In fact this happened before she left harbour and the meat had to be discharged.

The blow was too much for Mort, who had put a great deal of his own fortune into the venture and pinned his hopes on it. He died in 1878 at Bodalla, New South Wales, where a monument was put up to his memory.

As so often happens to pioneers, Mort's failure had laid the foundations of success. In May 1877—actually before his death—the *Frigorifique* sailed from Buenos Aires for Rouen with a cargo of meat, some of which, though not all, was landed fit for human consumption. A few months later the *Paraguay* left the same port with improved freezing apparatus and a cargo of mutton which, though on board ship for seven months, reached France in perfect condition.

In Australia experiments were pressed ahead meanwhile. A group of Queensland squatters chartered the *Strathleven*—a sailing ship, though carrying an auxiliary steam engine—which was fitted in Glasgow with a Bell-Coleman refrigerating plant and proceeded to Sydney, where she took on a cargo of beef, mutton and lamb. The beasts were killed ashore and the carcases frozen on board. The *Strathleven* cleared Port Jackson on the 29th November 1879, and entered the Port of London sixty-four days later, on the 2nd February 1880. It was a day that made history.

On inspection the meat was pronounced 'in a perfectly sound state, frozen quite hard'. It had been valued at $1\frac{1}{2}d.$ to $2d.$ a pound in Australia. On

Smithfield market the beef fetched an average of 5*d*. and the mutton 5½*d*. to 6*d*. a pound. A carcase of lamb was presented to Queen Victoria and a sheep to the Prince of Wales.

The Australian Frozen Meat Company was formed and chartered the *Protos*, which sailed towards the end of 1880 with 4,600 sheep and lamb carcases and 100 tons of butter. All this reached London in perfect condition in January 1881, at a time when the city was cut off from home supplies by heavy falls of snow. The meat fetched rather higher prices than the *Strathleven* shipment.

New Zealand had to face an even longer journey but was not far behind. The *Dunedin*, an iron ship of 1,320 tons gross, was fitted in Glasgow with a Bell-Coleman freezing plant like the *Strathleven*. She sailed in February 1882 with more than 5,000 carcases of mutton and lamb and some pork, and reached East India Dock, London, ninety-eight days later. Every carcase was inspected and only one had to be condemned. The rest were sent to Smithfield by night and were still hard frozen when the butchers came early next morning to buy. The whole lot were sold within a fortnight at an average of 6*d*. a pound (the mutton rather more and the lamb, strangely enough, a little less).

One farmer had consigned two sheep and three lambs direct to his son, an undergraduate at Jesus College, Cambridge. There they were cooked on the spit in the college kitchens. Next day the proud owner served cold New Zealand lamb at luncheon to the crew of the Jesus boat, which was then head of the river. One oarsman consumed three helpings.

So, within four years of Thomas Mort's death, the bulk shipment of meat from both the Antipodean colonies to Britain was an accomplished fact—a 'prodigious fact' *The Times* called it.

This newspaper's files for the year 1882 provide quite a documentary on the subject. In April—referring exclusively to Australian meat, the *Dunedin* being still at sea—it announced that the London and St Katharine's Dock Company had prepared roomy vaults with refrigerated chambers able to hold 8,000 carcases. These had been visited by a number of distinguished gentlemen, who witnessed the reception of a consignment of mutton, 'wrapped satisfactorily in canvas . . . the flesh being as pink and the fat as white as that of a sheep killed only a day'.

The *Dunedin*'s arrival created the greatest interest. It was greeted on the 27th May in a long leading article as 'such a triumph over physical difficulties as would have been incredible, and even unimaginable, a very few years ago'. 'It is impossible to say,' the writer went on, 'where this will end and how it will affect the destinies of this country'; and he hinted at impending changes in the status of the landed aristocracy and in the balance of employment in England, and a possible increase of emigration.

Letters to the Editor flowed in for the next two weeks. The Agent-General for New Zealand took occasion to assure the public that his country meant to send the Mother Country plenty of meat, and suggested that it was much better for England to receive food from her own kith and kin than from foreigners. Much of the correspondence revealed a deep-rooted prejudice against imported meat which was largely due to the fact that American beef had already, in some cases, been sold as English. The Duke of St Albans demanded fair play for the English farmer, who feared a fall in the price of his own product. A London butcher fairly let himself go, describing some of the letters as 'stupid twaddle', abusing the quality of imported meat in unmeasured terms, and dismissing cold storage as 'a bankrupt idea that had been proved by its failure to be impossible'.

The matter was also raised in the House of Lords. Lord Lamington wanted to know what the Government was going to do about it—a question which is always the last resort in puzzling circumstances. Lord Sudeley, for the Government, gave a reply which was characterised as unsatisfactory by the Duke of Rutland, who went on to advocate support for English agriculture which, he said, was 'in a depressed, not to say an alarming, condition'.

Developments

Most of this was the kind of thing one expects whenever some new portent appears on the horizon: many people are scared by its very unfamiliarity. But the most optimistic predictions were soon exceeded in sober fact. What those gallant little ships carried in their holds was indeed revolution—a change more direct in its results than political revolution and infinitely more beneficial to millions on both sides of the world.

In the late 1870s the proportion of imported meat sold on the London market was about 14 per cent of the total: in 1924 it was 76 per cent: by 1938 it was 80 per cent. This is not the whole picture, since only a part of Britain's meat passes through Smithfield; and, in general, the farther you go from London the less imported and the more home killed you find being sold. The figures for the country as a whole show different proportions but the same trend. In 1938 imported meat exceeded home killed in the ratio of roughly nine to eight. This was about the peak for meat imports. Since the second world war British farmers have increased their production dramatically, and they now supply almost three-quarters of the total.

During two world wars imported meat played a vital part in feeding civilians at home and the armed Services all over the world. Experiments have shown that the difference between fresh and properly frozen meat, in nutritive value and digestibility, is negligible. As to goodness—some British housewives still insist on 'Canterbury' lamb under the impression that it comes from Kent!

The benefit to consumers was no greater than the advantage to the producing countries. New Zealand's economy, at a low ebb during the early 1880s, took an upward turn as meat rose quickly to top place among the country's exports. Its sheep population, already large because wool was a staple product, rose by three million in ten years, and the value of every animal increased. Farmers changed their breeding policy. The merino sheep, noted for the finest and costliest wool, was crossed more and more with various English breeds, producing an animal that combines good wool with a heavier carcase. Today New Zealand exports more mutton and lamb than any other country in the world. To Britain she now sends about 20 million carcases a year.

In Australia developments took a different direction. Here large areas (like comparatively small parts of New Zealand's South Island) are most suitable for the hardier merino, and wool still takes a higher place in the country's export trade than mutton. Beef production, though very large, has been affected at intervals by serious droughts; while Australia's own rapidly growing population absorbs an increasing quantity. Nevertheless Australia, though never rivalling New Zealand so far as lamb is concerned, is among the world's great meat exporters. Her exports to all countries in 1961 amounted to more than 163,000 tons of beef

Swagman

and veal, 44,000 tons of mutton (mostly boned out and packed in cartons), and nearly 21,000 tons (say 1,350,000 carcases) of lamb.

While the frozen meat trade grew, the equipment and organisation to deal with it was built up. All around the coastlines of both countries there appeared works where the animals were killed and their carcases prepared and frozen for shipment; these, in the early days at any rate, were promoted and owned by farmers' co-operatives. Many of the old boiling down works were converted for the new and more productive process. In 1891—within ten years of the *Dunedin*'s first voyage—New Zealand alone had 17 export freezing works with a total capacity of more than $3\frac{1}{2}$ million carcases per year: today there are 33. There has been continual progress in hygiene, and in the inspection and grading of meat, so that the butcher thousands of miles away can be sure of getting what he wants and what he pays for. The shipping companies played their part by providing a regular service of refrigerated vessels; while the receiving ports and main markets were equipped with cold stores where thousands of carcases could be held, for months if necessary, in perfect condition.

Between the freezing works and the cattle and sheep stations buyers made their adventurous journeys, sometimes many hundreds of miles from base, into the Australian outback, making friends with graziers (as farmers are termed in Australia), talking over weather and prospects and the state of the market, bargaining for stock by the hundred or by the thousand. Gradually a complex organisation was evolved to establish prices according to supply and demand, and to ensure a square deal both for the farmer on one side of the world and for the butcher and his customers on the other. The key man is still the buyer, who must not only be able to estimate the dressed weight and skin value of every animal, but also needs to keep the confidence of the farmers, whom he refers to, and thinks of, as his 'clients'.

One link in the chain of production and marketing is a person whose existence is probably unknown to most people in Britain, though he is indispensable to the farmer: the stock and station agent. This person—this very substantial establishment in many cases—serves the farmer not only (as his title implies) as agent when land, buildings and livestock change hands, but also frequently as banker, providing finance for everything he requires to start up in business, including such necessities as fencing and implements. Thus he retains a real interest in the farmer's affairs. He continues as adviser, giving the benefit of his experience both of stock raising and of the market. In Australia at least he is generally present when the grazier sells livestock. In fact he is the farmer's guide, philosopher and friend, and an essential component in what economists call the price mechanism.

In the season a vast stream of livestock moves from the stations to the freezing works, from Central and Western Queensland and the Northern Territory to Brisbane, Rockhampton, Bowen, Townsville and Cairns, all ports on the East Coast. The distance may be over 1,000 miles. The drovers and their men walk the mobs over the first part of the journey, to the rail head. These drovers are, in the main, experienced men. The droving trips can at times be equal to half the total journey; the cattle then have to travel up to a further 600 miles by rail to the coastal meat works.

One drover, Jack Carroll, has taken one and, on some occasions, two mobs each year over the last fifty-odd years from Rocklands Station in the Northern Territory to Tanbar in the famous Channel country of South-West Queensland, a trip of eleven weeks and some 700 miles.

In recent years the pattern in Australia has changed with the improvement of outback roads. Large motor transports hauling three trailers carry thousands of cattle to rail heads. But still we see the drovers in charge of large mobs, for the cost over long distances is less. So the drover is still, like the stock agent, an important link in the chain.

The price of livestock has always been influenced not only by weather, which can drastically affect the supply and may also determine the time and the price at which the farmer wants to sell, but also by the market for wool and hides. The question of by-products in general has come to take an increasingly important part in the economics of the business, thanks largely to the discoveries of science. Today the freezing works supply materials to manufacturers of tennis rackets, buttons, fertilisers, glue, upholstery, artists' brushes, drugs, and surgical ligatures (these are only examples); and it is said that no part of an animal is unused except the moo and the baa. This benefits the farmer because it increases the value of his beasts, and the consumer because it reduces the selling price: the exporter, reckoning on some profit from by-products, can afford to pay more for livestock while charging less for meat.

One other development must be mentioned. Many experiments have been made in chilling as distinct from freezing. This requires that the meat should be held at a higher temperature, in fact just cold enough to keep it in good condition. It has been applied chiefly to beef; because the difference between frozen and fresh lamb is so negligible that the extra difficulties and costs of chilling are hardly worth while. The temperature has to be held within very close limits (between about 29 and 29½ degrees Fahrenheit) throughout the voyage; and the beef quarters, not being frozen hard, cannot be stacked one on another but have to be hung, which requires special arrangements and occupies a great deal more shipping space.

The first shipment of chilled Australian beef left Sydney in 1894 in the *Port Pirie*. Although temperature was controlled by a thermostat, something went wrong and the meat had to be frozen down during the voyage. In 1895 the *Gothic* made two trips with chilled beef from Wellington, New Zealand, and these were successful—technically at least: financial results did not encourage further efforts at that time. The question was taken up again between the two world wars, with the added refinement of 'gas storage' to check the growth of mould. In 1934 a cargo of chilled beef from Brisbane was discharged in London in 'perfect chilled condition'. After this several ships were adapted for the process. Chilling was discontinued in 1939. It has been resumed again since the war and is now proved. Australia and New Zealand would use it a great deal more than they do today if the United States had not provided more profitable outlets for beef in other forms.

Because of the shorter distances, chilling, in the early days at least, favoured shipments to Europe from the Western Hemisphere. Imports of chilled beef to Britain from the United States reached 1,900,000 quarters in 1901. After this they fell off sharply to practically nothing by 1913 (though

beef imports rose again during the first world war—most of it in frozen form). During the early part of this century South America became easily the leading supplier of meat to Europe, and most of this was chilled. The position remains much the same today. In 1961 Britain imported 2½ million quarters of chilled beef from South America— many times more than the total of frozen beef received from Australia and New Zealand—and nearly 1½ million carcases of frozen mutton and lamb—rather more than from Australia, though nothing approaching New Zealand's enormous total.

Postscript

The fate of the historic little *Dunedin* provides a postscript to this chapter. She continued carrying frozen mutton and lamb from New Zealand to England until 1890, making nine voyages in all. Then she entered with three rival ships in a race home for a sweepstake of £50 a ship. It was to be the last voyage of her genial captain, Roberts, who took his little daughter with him. The *Dunedin* sailed from Oamaru in March with the usual cargo of meat and wool and a crew of thirty-four. She was spoken once on the way to Cape Horn; and that was the last that was ever seen or heard of her.

Only two contestants finished that ill-fated race. The remains of the fourth, the *Marlborough*, were found on the grim coast near Tierra del Fuego in 1911. Three skeletons lay on the poop deck, each with a rusty pistol at its side, and more skeletons on the main deck. The rest is silence. At least we have some starting point for conjecturing her fate. In the *Dunedin*'s case we have none.

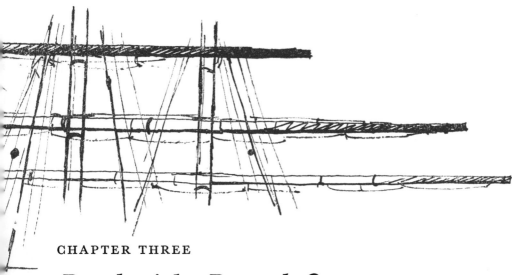

CHAPTER THREE

Borthwicks Branch Out

Thomas Borthwick was one of the first men in England to see the significance of the *Strathleven* and the *Dunedin*; and, being the man he was, he grasped the opportunity with both hands. Soon after his marriage his wife's two brothers and sister had emigrated to New Zealand and settled in the Waikato. One of them, Joseph Banks, was a member of the syndicate of New Zealand farmers who arranged the first shipment of meat to Liverpool; and there is a story current in Liverpool today that he offered the consignment to his father, who, feeling that he was too old to take on such a new venture, passed it on to his son-in-law, Borthwick. Another tradition is that when the shipment arrived the Liverpool wholesalers—showing the prejudice that was common enough at the time—refused to touch it; but when Thomas Borthwick was approached he replied in his broad Scots accent that he 'wouldn't mind trying it'. By such incidents are destinies decided; though, whatever the actual occasion, it is fairly certain that a man of Borthwick's character and views would not have stayed out of the business for long.

At all events it is known that in 1883—the year after the *Dunedin*'s first voyage—Thomas Borthwick was official selling agent for the New Zealand Loan and Mercantile Company. There is also an entry in the Mersey Docks and Harbour Board's records which shows that Joseph Banks sent him a shipment of frozen meat. A little later the firm was among the leaders in experiments with the chilling process: in 1895, when the *Gothic* made her successful voyages from Wellington, she brought 2,000 quarters of chilled beef consigned to Thomas Borthwick.

There is another tradition—this one was heard from a retired employee of the firm in New Zealand—that Borthwick, faced initially with a flat refusal by English butchers to handle frozen meat, hired a horse and trap and drove from door to door selling direct to housewives. Some doubt the truth of this on the ground that Borthwick was a wholesaler, not a retailer, and would deal in carcases and quarters, not in 'cuts'. On the other hand it is very much in character: and some butchers in those days did go round with 'cutting carts', cutting the meat up at the door to suit the customer. At any rate it illustrates how stories, credible and otherwise, grow round certain persons as they do round prophets of religion.

Expansion in Britain

In 1892 Borthwick bought No. 367 stall at Smithfield, and the eldest son, Thomas Banks Borthwick, then aged eighteen, came south to open a London office. This was in the Central Meat Market. It was soon outgrown and more roomy accommodation was found in West Smithfield.

One of the major difficulties to be faced in writing this book is the temptation to digress. This applies as much to Smithfield as it does to cattle stations in the sun-baked Australian outback, the magnificent sheep runs of New Zealand, the stock routes, the great auction sales, and the freezing works in both countries. Indeed these all belong. They are the scenery against which the story of Borthwicks unfolds. And in them character, atmosphere and history are inextricably intermingled.

History, in the case of Smithfield, goes back more than a thousand years. The place is first recorded as a 'smooth field'—hence the name—where the citizens of London used to gather for archery, tournaments, public executions and similar pastimes. Horses, cattle and other 'vendibles of the peasant' were sold there in the twelfth century. Smithfield was a recognised market before 1400, for in that year the market tolls were confirmed to the City of London by charter.

One would like to describe the present markets, built in the late nineteenth century (when costs were a fraction of what they are now) for £2 million, covering ten acres and containing nearly two miles of stall frontage, where more than 400,000 tons of meat, including pork and poultry, are handled in an average year; and the cold stores that can contain 600,000 carcases of mutton.

One would like to describe a day at Smithfield in a series of scenes, beginning at midnight when the 'pitchers' start unloading meat to the stalls and, later, between 4 and 5 a.m., the market staff proper—salesmen, clerks, cutters, porters, carriers—begin to arrive; the rush to get meat already on order cut up and away to the retail shops by the time they open; the really crowded hours when butchers and buyers come to make their own purchases, walking sagely from stall to stall, examining, selecting their choice— whole carcase, loin or hindquarter; English, Irish, Scotch, Australian, New Zealand, Argentine, Patagonian, Brazilian, Uruguayan, to which is added nowadays meat from South Africa, Rhodesia, Bechuanaland, Hungary, Yugoslavia, Holland, Sweden, Denmark and Iceland—bargaining over the odd farthing per pound (an important difference when you are selling thousands of carcases a day). All this is one stage of the endless process that brings good meat to the family table from pastures beyond the oceans in prime condition and at a fair price.

One would like also to speak of Borthwick's staff of the early days. Let us at least record the names of Bob Wilson, engaged as head salesman in 1895 soon after the London office was opened, who remained at 367 stall until he retired in 1935; and Arthur Savory, who started a little later and was salesman at another Borthwick stall, No. 137, for many years: he is remembered as a staunch supporter of the tradition that every well-dressed salesman must wear a straw hat.

One more picture from those times: the master himself (whose views on alcohol and efficiency have been mentioned) sitting on a stool outside one of the firm's Smithfield stalls with an eye on the door of the old Cock tavern and dismissing any salesman whom he saw entering or leaving those premises. If the man was a good worker Bob Wilson would often re-engage him and post him quickly to another stall.

London was now, in effect if not in name, the firm's headquarters. It was also, as it has been ever since, by far the most important centre of the imported meat trade in Britain. Any firm that was largely concerned in that trade had to be in London. It was obvious that Thomas Borthwick himself should not only visit but live there.

But was it so obvious? The question is worth asking because the answer to it involves the commercial creed of those times—a creed whose power and whose limitations we too easily forget today.

There were good reasons, which no doubt Thomas Borthwick saw at least as clearly as we can, why he should not move his home to London. He did not need to do so, for he was prosperous enough as he was. He had his house and his farm in the north, and most of his children were still at school there. He had always lived in the north, and the social attractions of the metropolis would be anything but attractive to a man of his character and views. He must have contemplated the change with the greatest reluctance. Why then did he go?

We may guess that he went because, according to his deepest beliefs, he had to go. He was one of that new class that grew up through the nineteenth century, composed of men who made their money in manufacturing and trade—the class that was challenging the old aristocracy for power, that was the backbone of the Liberal party which was soon to oust the Conservatives, the party of the landed gentry. The strength of that new class lay in the creed which it held with firm, fanatical conviction—the creed of *laissez-faire*, the 'power of the market place' and the survival of the fittest.

Thomas Borthwick with his Presbyterianism and his views on alcohol, betting and smoking was typical of that class. And, according to the creed to which he subscribed, to refuse such an opportunity on grounds of personal convenience would have been a moral weakness.

In its purest nineteenth-century form, the philosophy of *laissez-faire* is no more. Lord Keynes has driven his theoretical nails into its coffin. But its failure was practical. Like the mammoth and the mastodon, it met circumstances with which it could not cope; and then the sources of its strength—confidence, simplicity, reluctance to compromise or adapt—became its weakness. Today we see, perhaps too clearly, its ill effects. But for a hundred years—from Waterloo to 1914—it dominated Britain and the western world. And under its inspiration great things were achieved.

It was in 1895 that Thomas Borthwick brought his wife and young family to London and installed them in a house in Russell Square which he had purchased, presumably selling the Liverpool home. At the same time, the lease of the Welsh farm having expired, he purchased a small estate, Whitburgh, a few miles south of Edinburgh; thus coupling his favourite relaxation, farming, with a return (in spare time at least) to his native Scotland, which, though he had left it for business reasons, always kept its place in his heart. Whitburgh remains in the family's possession today.

In 1897 the two eldest sons, Thomas and James, were taken into partnership and the firm became Thomas Borthwick & Sons. From this time dates the use of the initials T. B. & S. which, enclosed in a diamond as a trade mark, have become so well known in Britain as also in Australia and New Zealand.

These various developments indicate a measure of prosperity and a great deal of confidence in the future. Money was evidently not in short supply and the business, though tiny by modern standards, was sound and expanding. This in spite of the butchers' prejudice against imported meat, which persisted remarkably, and was the reason for Borthwicks' venture into the retail trade. By 1900 they were running twenty-two shops in Liverpool, Glasgow, Hull and other towns. Later on this business was extended by the formation of a separate company under the name of John English. It was never a great success—no doubt because it was not undertaken from real conviction, being rather an instance of necessity met with determination. It was abandoned soon after the first world war. Since then Borthwicks' settled policy has been to keep out of the retail trade, and their guiding principle today is 'wholesale only'. This in Britain: in Australia and New Zealand, again for particular reasons, there are exceptions.

However, by the turn of the century Borthwicks had a substantial marketing organisation in Britain and—though they handled English and Scottish meat and some from other sources—their main effort was going into the selling of frozen beef, mutton and lamb from Australia and New Zealand. To this there was still considerable resistance, which came from butchers rather than from the public.

In Australia and New Zealand

Not a great deal is known of the firm's relations with the producing countries at this time. They worked at first, as in the case of the New Zealand Loan and Mercantile Company, as agents, taking a commission on each sale. When young Thomas Banks Borthwick went to Australia and New Zealand in 1898 his chief purpose, besides getting to know that end of the business, presumably was to persuade farmers, farmers' co-operatives and owners of freezing works to consign their meat to the firm of which he was now a junior partner. Soon, however—probably, in fact, before this visit—they started buying carcases delivered to the wharf; in which, of course, there was both greater potential profit and greater risk, with a corresponding increase in the capital required. After this again they began to buy live beasts, which were killed and prepared for shipment at the local abattoirs and freezing works for a payment of so much a head (an arrangement which is not uncommon today). Each method gave way to another gradually and they all overlapped. The firm certainly had their own livestock buyers working before 1900, and records show that they had an office in Ashburton, in the South Island of New Zealand, before 1903, by which date it was moved to Cashel Street, Christchurch—both places in the Canterbury district which was famous in England for its lamb even then.

After this developments came thick and fast. These must be kept for another chapter.

Other Sources

Borthwicks were not inactive in the trade with the Western Hemisphere. For a time they held the United Kingdom agency for the great American firm of Swifts: but this came to an end when Swifts started their own market-

ing organisation in Britain, by which time in any case imports from North America were very much on the wane, while South America was rapidly becoming Europe's chief supplier of imported meat. Borthwicks sent a representative to Buenos Aires in 1901 and he secured the agency for the La Blanca company's chilled and frozen beef and mutton. William, the third son, also paid a visit to South America, where incidentally he met the lady who was to become his wife and the mother of some of the next generation.

The La Blanca agency must have added considerably to Borthwicks' turnover. In 1905 it brought the largest cargo of meat ever shipped from South America. But it only lasted until 1908 when Armours bought the La Blanca company. This ended for ever the firm's direct connections in South America; although nowadays Borthwicks sell useful quantities of South American chilled beef on a commission basis, and buy lambs from Patagonia in most years.

The loss was looked on at the time as a major setback. Later on, when the firm had sufficient resources, it might have opened up in the Argentine. But it did not do so, perhaps because there was quite enough to think about in Australia and New Zealand. Today, considering Argentina's history of economic trouble, political unrest and dictatorship, Borthwicks are on the whole grateful for whatever circumstances kept them away.

Saleyards

CHAPTER FOUR

Twelve Years in the Southern Hemisphere

From now on the writer faces a fresh problem: how to recount coherently a rapid succession of events which take place on both sides of the world simultaneously, all interdependent and closely linked? The best way, for the coming period at least, will be to take a trip to Australia and New Zealand and to stay there watching developments for some twelve years or so. There will be plenty to keep us busy. In fact this is going to be a rather long chapter. Meanwhile we must not forget that things are happening in Britain at the same time.

Thomas Banks Borthwick's journey to Australia and New Zealand in 1898 was not his last. And his example was soon followed by his younger brothers. Their frequent visits had the object of consolidating and expanding the firm's interests in the countries from which its main supplies were drawn. They did so most effectively, not only by starting new enterprises, but also by personal friendships, and more than friendships, which produced branches of the family in both countries. James found his future bride in Australia; Algernon found his in New Zealand. The family is proud of its connection with the pioneer families in both countries.

And here another digression is inevitable. That word pioneer means so much. Further, it means one thing when referred to Australia and something else in connection with New Zealand. The habit of lumping these two great dominions together as 'the Antipodes' or 'Australasia' is convenient for brevity, but it is sadly misleading if it glosses over the enormous differences between them—differences in size, climate, scenery, economy, and not least in the character of their people; and to ignore these differences would be to miss an important component in this story.

The main factor affecting character is climate: it is still true today that it is more arduous to make a living from the land in Australia than in New Zealand. Some believe the two peoples spring from quite different stock, but this is not entirely true. Australia had its share of middle-class immigrants in the early days: there was a South Australian company which would only accept settlers with a reasonable capital backing just as happened in New Zealand. It is a poor joke to suggest that most modern Australians, those of British stock—for thousands of immigrants have come from the continent of Europe, particularly in recent years—are descended from the transported convicts of Botany Bay. Even where true, it should be a matter for congratulation. Among those convicts were many political prisoners, men of education and high ideals whose only offence was that they chose to think for themselves and to act on what they thought. Further, the convicts in general, whatever the cause of their transportation, produced in their immediate descendants—the currency lads and lasses as they were called—a remarkable race, a new type, realistic, sparing of words, self-reliant, extremely tough, and proud with a pride that was peculiarly their own. They contributed something unique to the country's development. It would be a sad day for Australia if that strain were to die out or its qualities become softened down by modern civilisation.

On the other hand it is certainly true that the early New Zealand settlers (who of course arrived much later than the first Australians) included a high proportion of solid middle-class people who brought with them—besides their strength and resolve—some capital, considerable resources, and a habit of political thinking which enabled them to work out for themselves, in a comparatively short time and in response to the conditions in which they found themselves, a system which, though showing its British ancestry in many respects, is without parallel in the world.

As to that word pioneer: if you want to know what it means, the best way is to look at some of the country. Start with a thousand miles or so of Queensland and the Northern Territory of Australia. Travel today is easy and comfortable: air services are plentiful and excellent; everyone uses them. In the dry season you will not see a green leaf the whole way. Everything is a reddish brown. The sun is relentless. Those little squares that reflect the sky are reservoirs—'tanks' they call them—which someone has dug and banked with great labour; unless they are very recent, in which case power-driven tractors and scrapers were probably used. With luck they will hold enough water to keep the cattle alive until the next rain. If not, the cattle will soon be dying. Here and there a deep well has been sunk and equipped with a pump and a windmill to drive it. But drilling is an expensive business, and you may go down 300 feet through rock and not find water. Despite the great benefits that artesian and sub-artesian wells have brought to Australia, no complete answer has yet been found to the problem of water in Queensland and the Northern Territory. When it is found, the productivity of these enormous expanses will be incalculable.

Roads are few but good. Every few miles your car slithers down the steep bank of a 'creek' (that is, the bed of a stream), bumps over the dry stones and climbs the other side. When the rain comes every creek will be full and the road impassable.

There were no aeroplanes when the pioneers came, and no roads and no tanks; only the bush and the kangaroos and giant lizards, and the enormous distances, and the sun and the water problem. The blackfellow might tolerate a stranger or he might kill him. It was here—and in other vast expanses far away in the north, south and west, all different but all hard, hot and hazardous—that Australia's magnificent cattle and sheep industry was founded and built up. The pioneers were tough.

Even today the outback is no bed of roses. Consider the life of a pumper— the man who is stationed at a bore during the hot, windless summer to ensure that the engine keeps running and that the tank is full of water for the thirsty cattle to drink. The cattle have eaten out the country around the bore, so that the prospect is usually barren as far as the eye can see. Some of the older men like this existence and eagerly accept a job as pumper. Perhaps they are the wise ones. But it could hardly be described as the height of civilisation.

Outback life has always been lonely and hard. Its law is the survival of the fittest. Luck plays a commanding role in the life of men in such a climate. Stability has come about through the expansion of the meat industry and its associated trades. The doors of the freezing works are open in any weather and a market exists for livestock even if drought-stricken. This certainly has reduced the old risk of ruin. The outback has become a better place to work and live in: even the social life and recreation have improved with the introduction of station air strips and the radio.

A typical New Zealand landscape cannot be compared with anything else; perhaps it is most like parts of Scotland, though on a grander scale. The hills, seen against a blue and white backdrop of snow-capped peaks, are steep and rounded and carpeted with rich smooth green. They are dotted with count-less sheep (English and Scottish breeds, or New Zealand's own part-merino cross, the Corriedale) plus a fair sprinkling of cattle.

These hills were not always like this. You can see others in their natural state. They are covered from top to bottom with forest—'bush' as in Austra-lia but in many places very much denser; thick-boled tree ferns and hard-woods such as totara and rimu, in parts as matted and impenetrable as a tropical rain forest. Some of this is preserved. Other areas are being con-verted to pasture now. Aeroplanes and aerial top-dressing to encourage the grass make the process incredibly quick and effective.

The pioneers penetrated this country on foot with pack-horses to carry their worldly goods, and cleared it with axes. That is how the first of the world's finest sheep pastures were made.

What changes the country has seen within a century! But how you assess the transformation depends on how you look at it. Compared with Australia, New Zealand today is a pair of cosy little islands with many modern com-forts but no very large towns. Compared with Britain, it still offers a prospect of great open spaces, fresh air, unlimited elbow room and opportunity for young people in whom the adventurous spirit survives.

Certainly when Thomas Banks Borthwick paid his first visit there before the turn of the century excitement had not been driven away by civilisation. He had a taste of it before ever he set foot in the country. The steamer in which he was crossing from Australia met heavy weather and lost her one and only propeller. They drifted helplessly for days in the Tasman Sea. Without wireless, they had no means of summoning help; though there was a cable and they knew they would have been reported overdue. The ladies on board set to work embroidering the ship's position on flags which were launched on little rafts every half hour. The issue of fresh water had been stopped immediately except for drinking. As they drifted towards New Zealand volunteers were called for to sail a lifeboat there and summon help.

This proved unnecessary. They were eventually found by a tug and towed into Wellington none the worse. Thomas Banks Borthwick, telling the story long afterwards to one of his nephews, said that it had really been rather fun.

However, the toughest of the pioneering days were over long before Thomas Borthwick's young sons came to Sydney and Wellington. The great

Australian desert kept the bones of its early explorers; others had followed their trails, and now a telegraph cable stretched across it from Adelaide to Darwin and on beneath the sea via Singapore to England. The magnificent coaches of Cobb & Company with their teams of matched horses carried travellers daily between the towns of Victoria, New South Wales and Queensland. Gold, after the chaos of the rushes, was an organised industry, and other minerals were making their contribution to the country's wealth. Buyers came from all over the world to the great wool auctions in Sydney. Cattle and sheep went to the freezing works in their seasons in an endless procession. With the growth of industry, and in the mines particularly, organised Labour was beginning to feel its power; and in the Federal Parliament in Melbourne (the latest step forward: it was opened in May 1901) England was being told in blunt terms to let Australia alone—in spite of which there was no disposition to scorn British capital or British export orders. The pull-devil-pull-baker for power between the Federal Government and the States was beginning. The States on the whole preferred to continue their old rivalry without an umpire.

In New Zealand the last of the bloody Maori wars had ended thirty years since, and white and brown were settling down to a kind of co-existence with equal opportunity which has no parallel in the world. Here too gold rushes had given way to a gold-mining industry; roads, railways and telegraphs were spreading their networks over both islands; and trade unions were forming themselves on British and Australian models. Parliament in Wellington, following nobody's model, was working away at a structure of laws which, though not founded on Socialist theory, turned out to be socialistic in character, and which was to have its influence on the future development of commerce and industry.

Both Australia and New Zealand, each in its own way, were embarking on the twentieth century with some confidence and some independence of thought; and both, with their economies unquestionably founded on expanding agriculture, knew well enough how much depended on exports.

Borthwicks' first freezing works

Borthwicks' first big step was to acquire freezing works of their own. The importance of this decision needs little emphasis. The firm was taking upon itself virtually another business, another link in the long chain of meat supply. It was putting itself in a stronger position to ensure regular deliveries to butchers' shops and homes in Britain and—equally important—to give better service to the farmers, for whom it is always vital to dispose of their stock at the right time. It was making no small investment in the producing countries and strengthening its ties with them.

The process, of course, was gradual. Borthwicks continued to use other freezing works under the old arrangements—most of them, in fact, at one time or another; for they were buying stock wherever stock was available, and the beasts had to be killed and prepared for shipment at some place within reasonable distance. They do so even today on a very considerable scale; their good relations with the 'outside' works are valued as an important asset and indeed an integral part of the business.

One can imagine the brothers travelling around, covering great distances in the days when neither aeroplanes nor motor-cars were to be had and the roads were not what they are today. It was a big responsibility for men so young. They were making decisions involving substantial expenditure in a business of which they had no direct experience. But they chose well. All the works mentioned here except one are still in the company's possession; and—though there have been plenty of problems and not a few emergencies—they give cause for no regret and much pride. The only regret is for the one that was wiped out irretrievably by what is legally called an Act of God.

The first purchase was at Waitara, in the Taranaki, on the west coast of the North Island of New Zealand. The place has its own character and history. A few miles away is New Plymouth, settled by people from the West Country who brought the name with them along with their accent and traditions. Both towns figured in the Maori war of 1860.

Borthwicks bought the works from the Waitara Freezing & Cold Storage Company in 1902 for £20,000. They had not run it long when the whole place was destroyed. Fire started late one night in the wooden supports beneath the corrugated iron roof of the engine room. Next morning nothing was left but a smoking ruin. It was a depressing sight for the townspeople, many of whom depended on the works for employment—except one man who was seen dancing a *haka* in the street. He was an insurance agent who had persuaded his company to refuse to cover the works.

That was in July 1904—the off season, fortunately. A quick reconstruction was done and the works was in operation again the following January. From that time Waitara was hard at it and the killing figures increased from year to year, except one season about 1908 when there was a bad slump in the trade and it was closed down. The area from which it was buying livestock in those days stretched from Otaki, on the west coast only 47 miles north of Wellington, to Maungaturoto beyond Auckland, and as far east as Opotiki on the Bay of Plenty.

The works stands on the Waitara river and had its own wharf. At that time, and for some fifteen years after, the frozen meat was carried by lighters to ships anchored out in the roadstead off New Plymouth. One day bad weather blew up quickly and a ship had to weigh anchor in a hurry, abandoning two lighters which had been unloading. These had no means of propulsion. When the storm cleared they were nowhere to be seen. They were found eventually somewhere north of Auckland, having drifted at least 400 miles. The men aboard had water and canned meat and were none the worse for their experiences.

The first investment in Australia was at Portland, in south-west Victoria. Portland, like Waitara, has character and associations. The oldest permanent settlement in Victoria, it stands on a small headland at one end of a bay, giving a strong impression (not supported by the maps) that you are as far south as you can get on the Australian mainland, looking straight over the southern horizon towards the Pole, preserving with quiet pride (and with great industry on the part of some senior inhabitants) memories that revolve round the old sealers and whalers and the historic name of Edward Henty. It is strongly reminiscent of coastal towns in New England—a name which the Portland district might well claim for itself. As it is you will find a Tintagel, a Redruth and a Marazion not far away: which, with Portland itself, indicate a close kinship (through West Country origins) with New Plymouth and the Taranaki in New Zealand. A strange coincidence.

None of this must be taken as suggesting that Portland is a sleepy place. It is noticeably up-and-coming. At the present time its big new harbour, only opened in 1960, is the subject of further improvements which, incidentally, will be of great benefit to its oldest surviving industry and mainstay, the freezing works.

This had been operating for about ten years (there were boiling-down works here long before that, first for whales and then for cattle and sheep) when Borthwicks bought it in 1905. Its previous owner was the Portland & Western District of Victoria Freezing Company, which was incorporated in 1894: its list of shareholders includes many names that have been well known in the district for a century or more. The purchase price is recorded in the old company's minutes as £16,500—a considerable sum for those times, though ridiculously small compared with today's money values. These minutes also mention discussions with N. W. Kingdon, who was Borthwicks' first general manager in Australia, and was evidently already a tower of strength, as he continued to be for some five years. After that he went to New Zealand for Armours. But he left a son, Nils, who is a senior buyer in the Mount Gambier area west of Portland.

The tremendous effects on Borthwicks of their investment in freezing works have been referred to. But these were not thought out in advance. The first moves were made because the opportunity happened to offer—that it offered in New Zealand and Australia within three years was mere chance—and because there were reasons against refusing. Both Waitara and Portland had already been selling their output through Borthwicks. Then the two companies that were running them found that they were not making enough money to satisfy their shareholders. So they each offered their works to Borthwicks; whose main motive in accepting was to ensure continuity of their supplies which might otherwise go elsewhere.

As so often in this story, an important step was taken because it seemed the thing to do in the circumstances of the moment. The fact remains that other men would have reacted differently. It must have been clear enough that they were embarking on something big; and their resources were limited. They might have drawn back. In that case there would probably be no story.

At the same time negotiations were in hand for 77 acres of land at Brooklyn, on the edge of Melbourne and some 200 miles east of Portland, which was also bought in 1905. This was the site for the first freezing works actually built by Borthwicks. It went into operation in 1908, starting modestly and working up until in 1914 it was killing 5,200 sheep and lambs per day plus a record quantity of beef. (This, it must be admitted, was due to a bad drought which put the farmers in a hurry to sell. But it has more than doubled those figures since.) Brooklyn, apart from its big capacity and the fact that it serves a very large farming area, has a special status in its nearness to the firm's Australian head office in Melbourne, and also to the famous auction sales of Newmarket, the largest in the Southern Hemisphere, where as many as 100,000 head may change hands in a single day.

Still in 1905 (old Thomas back in London must have needed strong nerves that year when he read his sons' reports; though perhaps it is just as likely that he was driving them along) Borthwicks started building another works. This was in New Zealand, in the beautiful Hawkes Bay area, on the opposite side of the North Island from Waitara. The place, which is called Paki Paki, is a few miles inland from the town of Hastings. The works itself must be spoken of in the past tense, having been wiped off the map by the Act of God already referred to. That incident, however, belongs to another chapter. For a good many years Paki Paki played its part in the firm's growing operations. For its buying area it had all the plains bordering Hawkes Bay, the hills that rise behind them towards the grim volcanic peaks of Ruapehu, Ngauruhoe and Tongariro, and all the lands to the north whose rivers flow into the Bay of Plenty. And it had the excellent port of Napier close at hand.

There were still vast productive areas beyond reach of any of Borthwicks' own works. In Australia there was the whole of Queensland for one. The firm had its team of buyers there of course, and there were abattoirs and 'outside' works at Brisbane and other places which were being made good use of. But things, once started, were not to be done by halves. A site was available at Murarrie, a few miles down river from Brisbane; and this was investigated by William Borthwick, accompanied by George Croll, the firm's superintending engineer for both Australia and New Zealand. The story is told with some relish in the works today, how those two crawled on their hands and knees over nearly a mile of waterfront that was covered with iron-bark and dense lantana scrub. However, they were favourably impressed. The great point was the river. Apart from Waitara in New Zealand this would be the first of Borthwicks' works that could load at its own wharf, thus avoiding the expense of double handling. And here there would be no lighters: the Brisbane river is accessible to ocean-going ships.

So the site was bought and named Moreton. This was in 1909. For some reason building did not start till near the end of 1910. It was completed and the first shipment made in 1912.

Today Moreton is no longer the only Borthwick works in Queensland. Another, at Bowen, a long way farther north, was acquired many years later. Both have been progressively extended and modernised—the technical changes in recent years have been revolutionary—so as to play their full part in the State's development. Moreton, besides being a big employer of local labour, supplies meat to the surrounding districts through the local trade—which in turn helps to provide year-round employment for more men. Until his retirement in 1962 its operations were under the control of A. A. van Homrigh, Brisbane branch manager for more than twenty years, and one of the firm's ablest and most devoted men.

The next major area to receive attention was the South Island of New

Zealand. Here a site was found at Belfast, near Christchurch. It was inspected by Cuthbert Harper, Borthwicks' first general manager in New Zealand, and his young assistant, E. G. Norman, recently arrived from England (who himself became general manager at a later date). This was a top-secret operation. The two men dressed themselves up in deerstalker hats and walked over the ground carrying guns and cartridge bags, ostensibly looking for rabbits. Their report was favourable. The site was purchased a few years after Moreton. The works was planned and building begun in 1914. The first kill was in December 1916. It amounted to 3,000 head per day, a creditable figure for a start.

Belfast is still the only Borthwick works in the South Island (though of course there are arrangements—as there always have been—with other works, particularly to cover the important South Otago district, and also Southland, where the firm has recently opened a small office at Invercargill). It stands in the famous Canterbury plains, within easy reach of Christchurch, capital and market centre of the province, where at that time was the firm's New Zealand head office, and where is still the South Island headquarters; and it has quick access to the port of Lyttelton.

So when the first world war broke out Borthwicks had five works in operation—three in Australia and two in New Zealand—with another on the way. These were wooden buildings with none of the refinements and aids to efficiency that are taken for granted nowadays, and their daily 'kill' was generally small by modern standards. But they were as busy as they could be, and their part in the expanding meat export trade was considerable. A British family round the dinner table might not know the name of Borthwicks, but their butcher certainly did; and so did an increasing number of farmers in Australia and New Zealand who were eager to dispose of their stock at the right time and at a fair price.

Each works had two focal points—the slaughterhouse and the freezers. Butchering was on the old 'solo' system, each man killing and processing an animal from start to finish—a more demanding job than the modern 'chain' system (it is known as 'line' killing in Britain) whereby a number of men work as a team, each being assigned one part, perhaps no more than a few quick knife cuts, which can be learned in a comparatively short time. The solo butcher was a highly skilled man. He needed to be, for he was paid so much a head—$2\frac{1}{2}d$. for a sheep or a lamb, $1s$. for a pig, $1s$. $4d$. for a bullock. (These are the actual rates paid at Waitara, New Zealand, in 1905–6. Hourly workers received $7s$. a day for a six-day week, with overtime at $1s$.

PRO FORMA.

Account Sales, No.

of   213 Sheep   ex   "Duke of Westminster"

Sold from   16th November to 3rd December.   by

THOMAS BORTHWICK & SONS,

for account of   Whom it may concern   of

Shipping Weight, lbs.   12174   Account Sale Weight, net lbs.   11998

Dock Weight, gross lbs.   12424   Trade Allowances and Tares, lbs.   426

Mark.	Carcases.	Description	Remarks	Net Weight.		Price per 8 lbs.	£	s.	d.
				Stone of 8 lbs.	lbs.				
No. 72	107	Sheep		749		2/3	61	2	10
"	92	"		654	4	2/3	68	3	6
"	14	"		96	2	2/-	9	12	6
	213			1499	6				

> Messrs. THOMAS BORTHWICK & SONS take this opportunity of calling your attention to their charges on consignments of Frozen Meat as shown below (N.B.—total charge for sales ex ship 2% commission), which will be found to compare favorably with those of any other firm in the trade, and to their form of Account Sales, which gives full information as to weights, time of sale, &c.
>
> The firm devotes its attention wholly to the Frozen Meat Trade, and having, in 1883, opened up the Country Markets in Liverpool, Manchester and shortly afterwards in Glasgow, possesses the advantage of having the oldest connection in the trade, selling direct to butchers all over the United Kingdom. The country markets receive special attention under the personal superintendence of a member of the firm, resident in Liverpool. The senior member of the firm has carried on the Live Stock and Dead Meat business for over 30 years.
>
> A thorough and practical knowledge of all classes of meat and experience gained by long study of the markets, enable the firm to select the right moment to sell goods entrusted to their consignment.
>
> Members of the firm are on the market every morning at the commencement of business and consignors may rely upon their goods making full market value.
>
> Credits at Bankers will be opened by arrangement for from 60 to 75 per cent. of current market values in London.
>
> Bankers: THE LONDON & MIDLAND BANK, WEST SMITHFIELD, LONDON, E.C.
>
> Cable Address: "OVERDRAW, LONDON." ABC & A1 Codes used.

                                                                                        158 18 10

CHARGES.

Stamp Duty on Policy   6

Freight and Primage   ...   .

Storage and Landing Charges:—

    One Month's Management Rate on 12424 lbs. at ½d. per lb.   2 18 2

    Extra Rent (when incurred) at 20/- per ton per month or ¾d. per cwt. per day

Cartage and Market dues   at 6/6 per ton on 12424lbs (from New Hibernia Wharf Store)   1 10 2

Fire Insurance   ...   .

Interest   ...   .

Commission at 2% on £ 158 18 10 (Including Delcredere)   3 3 7

                                                                              10 15 0

E. & O. E.   £   148 3 7

297, 298, 275 & 148, CENTRAL MEAT MARKET, E.C.

London, 24th Dec., 1897.   THOMAS BORTHWICK & SONS.

Account Sales, dated 1897, found amongst old papers in New Zealand

Lord Whitburgh, Chairman, 1912–1950

A. M. Borthwick, the present Chairman, from a drawing by Michael Ayrton

Waitara Freezing Works, New Zealand, some time before 1904

The same Works today

Lancashire Cold Store, Liverpool, before the first world war

54

A Souvenir from France, 1914–18.
The beef is Horn brand exported from Bowen Works, Queensland, where this photograph was found

A mob of 700 cattle crossing the McIntyre river from Queensland into New South Wales

an hour.) But his earnings were high for those times. A man's daily 'tally' was 20 bullocks or 100 sheep.

There was a fine spirit of rivalry between men and between works. The same spirit in fact pervaded all the staff. There is a story (this from rather later times when output had been pushed up and solo butchering was a thing of the past) of a foreman butcher who rushed through the works one evening shouting at the top of his voice: 'I've done it. I've done it.' Asked what he had done, he answered: 'I've killed 10,000 sheep in a day.' Someone inquired sarcastically whether the men had done anything.

The women belonged to Borthwicks in spirit almost as much as their husbands. One of them, whose home had the only telephone in the district, has remarked that in those days it was impossible to have a bridge evening because of the continual shouting into the old-fashioned machine on calls to all points of the compass. These would be mostly concerned with the buying of livestock. One night, however, when her husband was out there was an emergency call. Bad weather had stopped the loading of a shipment and all the carcases must be returned to the freezers at once to keep them in condition. Would she take a message to the manager's house? The manager's house was some distance away: but the weather did not stop *her*. In the pitch darkness she fell into a box-thorn hedge, coming out a mass of prickles. Then a shoe came off in the mud: a lightning flash enabled her to retrieve it. She was a sorry sight when she delivered the message. The manager offered to take her home. She answered: 'Don't waste time on me. You get on down and get the vans back.' When he had gone she found her own way home.

Another wife remarked that a girl who took up with a stock buyer didn't take long to find out that she had made a bigamous marriage: her husband was already wedded to his job.

There was plenty of fun too. Every works preserves its memories of some humorist, now probably in his grave, who was always up to something. At Moreton, for instance, there was a ripe character called Blackguard Jack, an enormous Irishman whose instinct for mischief was equal to his size. The tales they tell of him—the things he did to his mates and the things they did to him in return—would make a Homeric saga. Unfortunately the best are unprintable even without the rich language.

Though earnings were good, employment did not last through the year. The killing season varied in date from one works to another according to climate; but on average it was only about six or eight months, including sheep, lambs, cattle and a varying but smaller quantity of pigs. For the rest of the year the men would find other jobs, except a few who might be employed helping to build new freezers or extensions to the works. This is one of the respects in which there has been a great improvement in recent times, thanks largely to the growth of the local trade.

Comparatively few by-products were preserved then. Most important was wool, followed by hides and skins. Tongues were sent to local canneries. Strangely enough there was no market for livers or sweetbreads. Inedible offals went into 'digestors' which separated the fat, or tallow; the remainder, mixed with ground bone and dried blood, was sold as fertiliser—'manure' in those less refined times. (These are generalisations. There were always differences in detail between one works and another and between Australia and New Zealand.)

Buying

The livestock buying organisations in both countries expanded steadily. The quantities they bought were governed only by the natural checks of competition and price: the sales team in Britain could sell all that was sent to them and were always avid for more. Hence it was that 'outside' works played—as they still do today—an essential part in the firm's operations. At one time or another over the years Borthwicks have had killing arrangements with most works; although, as the works changed hands or conditions altered, the firm has had to adjust its plans as best it could. The head offices in Melbourne and Christchurch which looked after all operations—buying, works programmes and shipments—had heavy responsibilities, though they were modestly equipped by modern standards. The Melbourne staff in 1910 totalled ten, with one typewriter and no female typist.

Buyers, though they had to consider requirements and market prices, had a good deal more freedom of action than they have today; for they were frequently out of reach of telegram or telephone. A dozen buyers for various firms would set off from Brisbane together—all having celebrated the start of the season and all properly merry—for all parts of Queensland. They would go by train to the railhead, where each would hire a buggy or a riding horse and a pack-horse and disappear into the outback, buying by the thousand head at a time, arranging with drovers to take each mob to railhead, and stopping at the first telegraph office on the way home to wire Brisbane the total of their purchases. This would be after two or three months in the bush, where travelling was slow and arduous. Even later, when they had cars, what roads there were were of gravel and were crossed by open culverts. One New Zealand buyer, setting out proudly in his T model Ford, had fourteen punctures in a day.

Another buyer, retired some time since, has described his job in those days as 'a gentleman's business'; meaning that he and his clients mixed their commercial dealings with consideration. A bargain would not be enforced if, due to an unexpected change of weather, the farmer thought he could do better by keeping his stock a bit longer. It was a case of mutual interest, after all. Perhaps they enjoyed a touch of the grand manner too. Many farmers, particularly the Queensland cattle kings, were wealthy men. They did big things in a big way and expected the same spirit in return.

Sometimes, when reports of demand from London were good, buyers would be told to 'get them'. Then they would go out and work from dawn to dark, each on his own. But this did not mean that price was of no consequence. A Canterbury buyer who allowed too much for skin values on a flock of lambs was told in the Christchurch office: 'We're buying meat, not wool' —a contrast with today when buyers are expert in the value of wool, pelt and hide, primed with current market prices, and estimating closely the weight and quality of wool on a sheep's back. Then as now, however, the buyer's judgment was crucial. Among other things he always had to consider the condition of the stock route and the length of the rail journey: for these affect the beasts' weight when they reach the holding pens at the works; and it is 'dressed weight' that matters.

Meat firms did a good deal more buying in the saleyards then. (This perhaps was because dealings in those days included a much greater proportion of wethers, which are less likely than lambs to get knocked about and damaged in the yards. It is interesting to see how the production of wethers has declined. In 1922–3, the first full year for which records are readily available, New Zealand exported over a million wether carcases: in 1961–2, little more than half a million. The corresponding figures from Australia include both wethers and ewes, which are all a by-product of the wool industry. They are—1922–3, 1,856,000; 1961–2, 47,000.) At the great auctions of Newmarket in Australia and Christchurch in New Zealand thousands of head would change hands on a nod.

The drover was a responsible link in the chain of supply. He was weatherwise; he knew how far the beasts could walk in a day without undue loss of weight, when they wanted a 'spell', how much feed and water were needed and where these could be found. He also had to consider their temperament.

Bullocks, if they are unused to being handled, can be particularly nervous. One Queensland drover, having taken a mob to the railhead for Brisbane, went to see, before turning in himself, that they were comfortably settled for the night and ready for trucking in the morning. He struck a match. The animals panicked. When daylight came he found them scattered four miles down the road.

A drover's responsibilities are roughly in proportion to the number of head and the distance: both of which may be considerable. From Rocklands,* a station rather far north on the border of Queensland and the Northern Territory, about 4,500 steers one or two years old, which are ready for fattening, are driven annually in mobs of 1,250 some 700 miles south to the fattening pastures of Tanbar, in the Cooper's Creek country. Cooper's Creek, incidentally, is a phenomenon. It is land-locked; and after the rains it spreads out over a flat expanse 150 miles wide. The Rocklands cattle are moved just in time to take advantage of this natural irrigation. In a few months they grow fat on grass alone. Then they spend another three weeks on the road to the railhead, from which they are trucked about 800 miles to the works. Contract drovers are paid today about five shillings a head for every one hundred miles.

Big purchases and big draftings are a favourite subject for memories of the early days. Borthwick men now retired in and around Brisbane still talk, when they get together, of the time when Pat Clarke bought 80,000 wethers in central Queensland. A man named Maskey was in charge of the droving teams. He was helped by his two sons. (One of them, Wally, was a buyer for the Brisbane office for many years afterwards.) They took them in 16 mobs of 5,000 each, 42 miles from Bowen Downs to the railhead at Aramac. If no trucks were to be had there (the line was being extended from Seven Mile Bore to Aramac during the operation) they went on to the next station. Then the sheep were taken by rail to Brisbane. The chief truckers' names too are remembered: they were Wally Cooper and 'Dummy' Yates. At Brisbane station Stan Stanley, head stockman at Moreton, took charge of them, and so they reached the Moreton works. The overall distance is some 600 miles as the crow flies: nothing compared with draftings from the Northern Territory but a good deal farther than from Aberdeen to London.

That was in 1914. It is thought to be still a record for quantity: big pur-

*In case this reference to Rocklands should give the impression that it is Borthwicks' property, it may be as well to mention that it is in fact owned by Rocklands Station Proprietary Limited, a company in which Borthwicks have a shareholding.

chases are fewer today because large estates have been broken up. But not for price. Money values have gone up so enormously. Higher figures have been paid on some single deals in recent times; for instance when six thousand bullocks were bought from Marion Downs at an average of more than £40 a head.

Borthwicks' first cattle station

In January 1914 Borthwicks acquired the leasehold of Banchory,* a cattle station some 400 square miles in area in the central district of Queensland, together with other leases which brought the total holding to 1,200 square miles. The negotiations, incidentally, were conducted by James Balderstone, a young man who had succeeded Kingdon as general manager in Australia.

It is a little breath-taking to find what was really quite a small firm, controlled by its founder and his four young sons (though evidently they had enlisted the support of very able men who knew the country and the business), taking on yet another new activity, another link in the chain of supply, within the twelve years that this chapter covers. But it was a sound if extremely courageous move. Borthwicks still have Banchory, though not the other leases which were originally attached to it. They also have two more cattle stations farther west, each more than twice Banchory's present size. These latter are different in character and climate, and fill a slightly different role in the complex machinery of meat production. The three together, though they only provide a fraction of the beef that goes into the two Queensland works, form a definite unit in the organisation, and one which is valued highly for a number of reasons. They help to secure an economic balance; if the works pay too much for stock and so lose money on the meat, at least the cattle stations will have profited by the mistake, and vice versa. They can guarantee a certain supply at any time the works want it, even when farmers have good reason to hang on to their stock. Further, they represent an interest which is essential to the firm and characteristic of the Borthwick family—an interest in farming and, particularly, in the breeding and fattening of beasts.

Banchory was given its name by two pioneers who set out in 1860 from Rockhampton to find somewhere to settle, reached the Never Never country,

*More space is devoted to Banchory and to cattle stations than their place in the scheme of things seems to deserve. This is simply because most people, leading a very different sort of life, enjoy reading about these things.

and chose this place. At least one of them must have been a Scot—no doubt the one whose name was John Muirhead. Many of that nationality were settling in the neighbourhood. They left permanent record of their origin in such place names as Blair Atholl and Islay; though Surbiton, not far away, tells of one who came from south of the Border. These facts suggest that the accents and characters that you will find in this part of Queensland will be different from those of, say, Portland or Waitara. Which is perfectly correct. The people are as different as the country. You soon find that a generalisation about 'Australia' or 'New Zealand' is as likely to be right as a generalisation about 'Europe'.

Banchory has seen changes. There are traces of gold mining round about. Muirhead and his partner stocked the place with sheep from Darling Downs and the Burnett which, as his diary shows, did very well. But cattle, for which the country is most suitable, were here long before refrigeration started, though the only exportable items they produced were hides and tallow; there was a boiling down works at Laurel Bank, near Rockhampton.

The original homestead had slits in the walls for guns to repel attacks by the Belyando, the local blackfellow tribe. It was replaced about 1895 by a comfortable building with a wide, cool veranda which became the home of successive Borthwick station managers and their families.

The big drought of 1902 killed off, it is said, the whole herd and the then owners abandoned the property, which was vacant for some years until it was taken on by Colonel Cope, a Sydney barrister, who re-stocked it. He used to sell bullocks to Borthwicks, who were impressed by his shrewdness in always keeping back the best until the spring when prices would be higher. When they bought the property he said to Balderstone: 'You'll be selling it back to me in a few years.' He was wrong. They put in a manager, Ted Tooker, introduced some pedigree bulls from New Zealand to improve the strain and, apart from some troubles, all went well.

Until the first T model Ford arrived after the first world war all transport was by pack-horse, dray or wagonette. One of Tooker's successors recalled that it took him seven hours and two fresh horses to drive the 42 miles from Clermont in a light buggy, crossing 42 creeks on the way. Clermont, the nearest railway station, was where the stock was trucked for Brisbane in those days. There was no telephone at Banchory and no mail delivery. The men were kept busy by a continual war against noogoora burr and prickly pear, 'insect' pests (the worst was the tick that carries red water disease), dingoes and 'poddy dodgers'—the Queensland name for cattle thieves.

Most important, there were no earth dams and no bores. The beasts lived, if they lived, through the dry season on surface water and shallow wells. On the other hand feed was never a major problem. To anyone brought up among the pastures of Devon or Midlothian it is a revelation how cattle find enough to eat, wandering in the heat between tall trunks of iron-bark and gum, picking at turkey bush, turpentine and cassia; brigalow and gidyea on the flats; box, river gum and coolibah along the creeks; and, as a last resort during the drought, the prickly and indestructible spinifex.*

At length the rain comes, and everything is green almost overnight; the Mitchell grass grows, and the beasts begin to fatten. They are slower to put on condition than those that crop the lush pastures of southern England or the feed lots of California. But the natural grasses are sweet and free from stimulants, and the beef they produce is as good as any in the world. An American cattleman visiting Australia described the beasts he saw there as 'tall as a horse, rangy, big boned, big framed, with lots of light under them'. This may be a fair description of cattle which before they are two years old have been driven for two or three months in tropical heat from breeding station to fattening property; but a Queensland steak grilled over the embers of a eucalyptus fire is as succulent as the dearest dish at Maxims or the Savoy. Incidentally the Banchory cattle—polled Shorthorn with some Devon blood—are thicker and lower set than most.

The property was not subdivided in those days. Apart from a bullock 'paddock' (a paddock may be any size) there was only a ring fence marking the boundary. The cattle were free to go where they liked. There was no 'culling' or 'speying'—the selection and de-sexing of bulls and cows which is now an annual routine. Once a year the stockmen would go out mustering as they do still. (Don't call them cowboys. The cowboy in Australia is the man who milks the dairy cows for the homestead and cuts wood for the manager's wife.) They are mounted, and have with them, besides camping kit, a bag of tea and a billy hung on the saddle. (Tea is as much a part of life in Australia as in England. Horses more so: besides racing—Melbourne Cup day is a public holiday in the city—they are still the best way of getting about in the bush. The stockmen's horses show the influence of breeding for racing.)

Having made their camp, the musterers sweep as large a sector of country as they can cover, and bring all the beasts into yards, separating the weanable calves which are later to be driven to the fattening pastures, branding, de-

*This is a general description. In fact no spinifex grows at Banchory.

horning, ear-marking and castrating. They are experts at these jobs. The American already quoted timed a four-man crew who did 65 calves in an hour. When all is done they work another sector. As soon as a whole circle has been worked they move camp and start again.

Banchory is only about 250 miles from the coast and has a comparatively high rainfall. Its average over ten years was $28\frac{1}{2}$ inches; though there were big variations, the maximum being 43 and the minimum 14. Its carrying capacity is high—18 head per square mile. Compare this with some stations farther west which never have more than ten inches of rain, sometimes less than four, and cannot support more than four head per square mile.

These stations together constitute yet another close tie between Borthwicks and the great meat producing countries of the Commonwealth. They are the firm's roots in the land.

Family ties

Meanwhile still closer ties were being forged by the family itself. Algernon's two sons were born in New Zealand of a New Zealand mother. In time both became directors of Borthwicks. The elder, now chairman of the company, will be called Algy here to distinguish him from his father; he is known universally as 'Mr Algy'. The younger, Pat, soon made his home in New Zealand, and is now the family resident director of the Australasian branch of the business.

Some Statistical Notes

Waitara Works, in the Taranaki district of the North Island of New Zealand, was bought from the Waitara Freezing and Cold Storage Company in 1902 for £20,000. Its book value today including all the extensions and improvements is just over £1 million. The annual kill nowadays is about 600,000 sheep and lamb and 45,000 cattle. A great many calves are also killed at this—as well as at most other—works.

Portland Works, in South West Victoria, was the first Australian acquisition. It was bought in 1903 from the Portland and Western District Freezing and Cold Storage Company. It was sold by the partnership in 1906 to the newly-formed T. B. & S. (Australasia) Ltd. for £16,000. Today it is valued in the books at over £A.500,000 and the kill is about 450,000 sheep and lamb and 15,000 cattle. By the way, £A.125 is equivalent to £100 sterling

Brooklyn Works, near Melbourne, Victoria, was the first works actually built by Borthwicks. In operation in 1908, it cost £A.28,700 and is valued in the books today with all its additions at just over £A.600,000. The kill today is some 800,000 sheep and lamb and over 20,000 cattle.

Moreton Works, Brisbane, completed in 1912, cost £A.115,000. The book valuation now is £A.600,000. The works kills each year about 50,000 cattle and 50,000 sheep.

Belfast (Canterbury) Works, New Zealand, was built between 1914 and 1916 and cost £111,000. Its book value today is getting on for £700,000. The original capacity was 300,000 sheep and lamb but nowadays its annual kill is in the region of 800,000 sheep and lamb and 15,000 cattle.

Throughout this story, one must bear in mind that all these expansions were paid for by money earned, taxed, then ploughed back into the business. The term 'valuation' in the books is expressly used as a revaluation of fixed assets was carried out in 1954: more about this on page 201.

Audrey House, Ely Place, London

CHAPTER FIVE

Twelve Years in Britain

Now we must go back in time; and in space we must return from sun-drenched pastures to the crowded streets and fogs of London. While that remarkable series of events was happening in Australia and New Zealand, developments were going on in Britain also; and these, though perhaps less colourful to describe, were no less important. While supply arrangements were being built up on one side of the world, the distributive network was expanding on the other. While so much money and effort was being put into freezing works and stock-raising, attention was also given to organisation and financial structure. The firm was growing: it was also, in some important respects, changing—not its character, but its system of control.

About 1902 (the exact date is not recorded) Thomas Borthwick's two younger sons, William and Algernon, became partners in the business. In 1905 the partnership ended and a limited company, Thomas Borthwick & Sons, was formed with an issued capital of £300,000. In addition to two Smithfield stalls (Nos. 148 and 367) and the office at 11 West Smithfield, the new company's assets included eight stalls in provincial meat markets, 1,000 one-dollar shares in Frigorifico La Blanca and a £45,000 investment in a wholly-owned subsidiary company, Thomas Borthwick & Sons (Australasia) Limited, which owned the works and conducted the buying operations in New Zealand and Australia. Thomas Borthwick and his sons owned the ordinary shares and at this time his daughters held the preference shares.

Here a question asks itself. Why a subsidiary company? And, if one subsidiary company, why not two, one for Australia and one for New Zealand? The answer, apart from administrative convenience, is one word—a word that goes far to account for many features of company structure today and was beginning to have its influence even then: taxation.

Borthwicks' activities in Australia and New Zealand until 1900 and a few years after consisted mainly in persuading farmers, dealers and owners of works to consign their meat to the firm in Britain for sale there. The only money they received from those people was their commission on sales. The total was not large and so far there had been no question of its being taxed in the countries from which it came. But the business was growing and taking on new commitments, freezing works in particular. Presumably its earnings in those countries would grow too; and the time was bound to come when the tax authorities in Australia and New Zealand would want their share. The subsidiary company was formed to ease such complications as might subsequently arise.

The idea of a single subsidiary covering both countries came from the quite correct belief that tax charged in Britain (T. B. & S. (Australasia) is an English company with headquarters in London) would be based on its total profits, and that if one country showed a profit and the other a loss the one could be set off against the other.

It was also assumed, rather naïvely as it turned out, that the same would apply to tax paid in Australia and New Zealand. This in fact was not an arrangement which commended itself to the tax authorities in those countries, particularly when the firm's activities there, and their earnings, grew to much greater proportions. As a result all sorts of difficulties and arguments arose. In the light of later experience the present directors of Borthwicks would probably have voted in favour of separate companies for Australia and New Zealand. All that can be said is that in 1905 that experience was still in the future, and the oldest of the present directors was in his cradle. Thomas Borthwick and his sons and advisers acted as seemed best to them at the time.

In the same year the London office was moved from West Smithfield to the ground floor of Audrey House, Ely Place. In this building the firm's headquarters remained (except during the second world war) until 1963; though later it was promoted to more commodious premises on the first floor. Ely Place is a cul-de-sac—which proved an increasing boon with the continual growth and grumble of traffic past its open end—and within a few minutes of the great meat market.

During the middle part of the period with which we are now concerned, the founder's four sons were—quite naturally and gradually—taking over control of the business. This, apart from expansion and the administrative measures required by expansion, was the greatest change that was going on between, say, 1905 and 1912. Whatever the reasons for converting the partnership into a company, it was certainly not that the next generation were reluctant to take on the running of it. Thomas Borthwick, and the firm, were extraordinarily fortunate in having four such men ready and willing to receive the baton from him.

What part is played in any success story by what we call chance? A successful man is one who seizes his opportunities. But what if opportunities fail to arrive? What, for instance, would be the story of Thomas Borthwick if he had not happened to have a brother-in-law who was in New Zealand when refrigerated meat shipment became a practical proposition? Then, again, good luck may appear in disguise and not be recognised at all until later. The loss of the South American connection seemed a big blow to Borthwicks at the time; but it turned out for the best. And now, what would have been the position if Thomas had had only daughters? Or, later, if the next generation had not included grandsons? There is more in this question than meets the eye (it gets involved with the tax question once again) and it will be considered in due course. Meanwhile the fact is that there were four sons. Their father no doubt took this for granted. No doubt also he assumed that they would all come into the business and spend their working lives in it. What else? Refinements of psychology and temperament would hardly occur to the Victorian merchant.

He was wrong about one of them. The third, William, had always wanted to go into politics. He stayed with the firm—until about 1910. Then at length he decided to follow his bent. He ceased to take any active part in running the firm's day-to-day affairs (though he kept his seat on the Board) and read for the Bar as a preliminary to a political career. This, however, was towards the end of the period with which we are now concerned. In the meantime he carried on and did his full share of the work, including visits to Australia, New Zealand and South America. So it is true to say that Thomas's four sons received the baton from him.

But, like all sons who have got something in them, they ran their own race. They were different characters. In particular they were collectively more cautious than their father. Not, of course, timorous: no further evidence is called for of this. But nature or adaptation gave them the qualities that were most needed to meet changing conditions. Thomas Borthwick was a pioneer. He had the temperament that a pioneer must have—sanguine, with very little respect for risks or difficulties. He had seen something like a vision; and he went for it without bothering too much about details. The legend that the old hold back the young was not true of him. He would have expanded much faster if he had had his way—exactly as fast as his banker would let him.

Some weaknesses or deficiencies in the firm's organisation must have struck the sons, who with true Scottish prudence—without in any way ignoring the call for further initiative—set about overhauling the machinery. If they had not done so, continued expansion would have resulted in a rickety edifice. As it was, Borthwicks were enabled to cope with rapid developments; developments which, spread over firms and individuals throughout the meat export industry, gave British people the plentiful supplies they enjoy today, and provided Australia and (still more) New Zealand with the means to strengthen their economies, preparing them for a general advance that is in striking contrast with the story of their closest rivals in the trade, the countries of South America.

The business of forming a limited company offered, among other benefits, an occasion for facing up to some necessary adjustments. This went on for a couple of years; and the auditors—Wederell, Trenow & Gillat—played their part in it with patience and application. They evidently had quite a job. Their letter enclosing the accounts for 1907 contained some significant remarks. For instance: 'It appears that the dividend on the preference shares was erroneously paid free of income tax . . . and there was additional remuneration due to two senior employees which had not been included . . . . We have found a considerable number of vouchers missing . . . . The majority of them have since been produced but there still remain a number of which we understand duplicates are being obtained.' And they add a tactful suggestion that 'some improved method of filing should be adopted to bring the vouchers more in line with the books . . . '. They also point out that the Board minutes for three dates in 1907 have not yet been signed by the chairman. Finally: 'If you will kindly advise us when the above matters have been dealt with we are at your service to complete the audit.' Patience indeed! But it was rewarded. They had no further cause to complain.

From then on the rate of expansion, though by no means slow, was governed not by what money the firm could borrow but by what it actually had.

As a result, by 1913 a bank loan had given way to a substantial credit balance; assets entered under 'goodwill' had been written off; and the proportion of current liabilities to current assets was greatly improved. Borthwicks now had their financial feet on the ground. They could face future opportunities, and future knocks, with assurance. Further advances were to be achieved by the patient policy of ploughing back.

Already the firm had gone into cold storage—in the technical sense, that is. At first they had used the public cold stores that began to spring up in Britain as soon as frozen meat shipment was proved practicable; just as they had used 'outside' abattoirs and freezing works in Australia and New Zealand. But in 1900 they took a thirty-five-year lease of Kennet Wharf, on the Thames, which was itself equipped with a cold store. For some reason this was run until 1920 as a subsidiary company, the Thames Cold Storage Company Limited. In 1907 a like venture was undertaken in Liverpool: the firm took over the lease of the Lancashire Cold Store, Canada Dock; and another subsidiary, the Lancashire Cold Storage Company Limited, was formed to run it.

Kennet Wharf was soon a hive of industry at all hours. Of its several managers in the early days one, John Hampton, is specially remembered. He had everything timed to the minute. Travellers would telephone their orders through, sometimes at midnight, and the meat would be cut up, loaded and delivered to butchers in the provinces by the time they opened their shops in the morning.

Borthwicks still operate the Lancashire Cold Store, now considerably enlarged. In fact, after London, Liverpool is the biggest centre of the firm's distribution network in Britain; as is appropriate for the place where Thomas Borthwick did so much of the work that laid the foundations of the business, and where so many stories of him are still in circulation. Much material for this record has been gathered there. Meat sales were conducted in the early days at the Trowbridge Street abattoir. In 1912 the Liverpool Meat Market was opened; and there of course Borthwicks had their stall until 1931, when there was another move.

At Smithfield expansion continued to meet the growth of supply and demand. In 1900 Borthwicks took another stall, No. 148, in the Central Markets. In 1910 another was taken, and in 1914 two more. These last three are still held by the firm.

There was development in the West of England. In the early years of the century this whole area was supplied from London, most deliveries being by rail. The firm had a one-room office in High Street, Bristol, over Singer's sewing machine shop—'a rat-infested hole' was the description given by one who later became manager of the Bristol branch. Then, in 1913, Borthwicks decided to ship meat into Avonmouth and to work the western district from there, using the Royal Edward Cold Store. Today Bristol, though not as big as Liverpool, is an important centre with three sub-branches, serving a wide area. Its daily road delivery service operates as far as Penzance.

The firm also started branches within the first decade of the century at Cardiff, Croydon, Kingston and Brighton.

During this time Borthwicks began to tender, in common with many of their competitors, for contracts to supply meat and offals to the Services. Invitations to tender were issued at regular intervals by the War Office and the Admiralty. This has gone on (except during the second world war when special arrangements were made) ever since, with the addition of the Air Ministry. Service contracts have always called for first-quality meat and there are rigid specifications as to fat covering, weight and cut. To cater for them efficiently calls for accurate market anticipation and careful regulation of shipments, both to Britain and to every part of the world where British units are stationed.

Mention must be made here of Frederick Swift, who joined the company in 1908. He became a director in 1923—the first of the very few who have not been members of the family—and died in harness in 1935.

One who started in the London office as a junior clerk at the age of twenty in 1913 (William Miles: he was office manager before he retired at the end of 1959) has described what it was like before the first world war. The clerks all wore morning coats and striped trousers. They sat on high stools at tall sloping desks, which faced both ways and seated three on either side. There was a similar desk, but single, for the manager of the country department. The latter was the 'living image' of Mr Pickwick, including his dress and his addiction to snuff. Telephones were of the wall type, with a handle that you had to turn to attract the attention of the exchange. The rooms were warmed by open fires which did not always give out much heat when the clerks came in on winter mornings. Work started at 8.30 a.m. and often did not finish until 9 p.m.

Once a week the staff were paid by Mr Twist, the company secretary, who sat in the general office. They were paid in gold—for Miles, one sovereign and one half-sovereign.

A story of Twist is told by a young man (young then) named E. G.

R. G. Bremner, London Director, retired 1959

*J. S. Balderstone, senior, Australian General Manager and Director,
retired 1945*

E. G. Norman, New Zealand General Manager and Director until 1956;
Director until 1961

Borthwick Wharf, Deptford, London,
from the landward side showing the loading bank for 'land carriage'

Borthwick Wharf from the river. In the foreground is the first refrigerated barge ever to operate on the Thames, one of a fleet specially built for charter to Borthwicks

A view of the Thames from Borthwick Wharf. These are the normal, insulated barges, which up to now—see page 77—have carried frozen meat between the ships and the riverside Cold Stores

The main avenue of Smithfield Meat Market, London. One of Borthwicks' shops, No. 89, can be seen at the far right of this picture

A market stall in Manchester

Norman, known now to everyone as Ted. He joined the firm in 1911 as a surveyor of meat. Twist paid him on Fridays by cheque. But his job took him all over the country—Bristol, Birmingham, everywhere—and often he was not back in London by Friday afternoon. Then he would go in on Monday and ask for his cheque. Twist would answer: 'Your cheque is in the safe. You'll get it next Friday.' Sometimes this went on for weeks on end until poor Norman was broke. He had to appeal to the head of the firm to get it put right.

On the other hand, a few years later, during the first world war, when Norman was in hospital in England, nobody could have been kinder to him than Twist. The secretary had uncompromising ideas about discipline but a warm heart.

The head of the firm by that time was the eldest son, Thomas Banks Borthwick—Lord Whitburgh he was then. There is another story about him and Ted Norman. One day in 1913 he sent for Norman and asked if he would go to New Zealand for the company. The young man wanted to consult his mother. Lord Whitburgh agreed but said he would expect an answer next morning. Next morning, a Thursday, Ted went back and said he would go. Lord Whitburgh answered: 'Good. I have got you a passage. You leave next Tuesday.'

Ted Norman went to New Zealand. His name has already cropped up in the previous chapter. He is still there, though now retired.*

Thomas Borthwick's last years

Thomas Borthwick was seventy when his firm became a limited company. He was not one to hold on to authority beyond his due time; and the right men were there to take over. Wiser than many successful business men, he had kept other interests alive. He was already beginning to give more time to his beloved Midlothian farm. In those days the main line trains between London and Edinburgh stopped at Tynehead, only three miles from Whitburgh; and he made good use of them. He spent the greater part of every summer there.

His attachment to his own soil and its people takes second place in this story, inevitably. But, having acquired land, he developed the real paternal devotion that is characteristic of the old-fashioned landed gentry. It was an

*In fact, he died in 1963 since this was written.

active devotion. He was a County Councillor of Midlothian for some years, Justice of the Peace, and (an appointment which came within a day or two of his death) chairman of the Midlothian National Insurance Act Committee. He took a great interest in technical education. Neither the preoccupations of business, nor his farm, prevented him from working for his county.

He also found time to take a practical part in national politics. He had always been a convinced radical. The Liberals ('Radicals' always to the opposition *Scotsman*) were staging a big come-back around the turn of the century, first under Gladstone and then under Asquith, leading up to their sweeping victory at the polls in 1906. Midlothian, a staunch Liberal seat, was Gladstone's own constituency for a long time, and his four Midlothian campaigns are historic. At any rate in the last of these, in 1892, Thomas Borthwick is said to have taken a conspicuous part. But it was in 1899 that his official connection with the constituency began. This was in support of his friend the Master of Elibank—one of the foremost in the brilliant group that surrounded Campbell-Bannerman and Asquith—who first won Midlothian in 1900. Borthwick became chairman of the Midlothian Liberal Association in 1902 and remained so until his death, travelling many miles to preside at party meetings in the county.

After the great pro-Liberal landslide of 1906 he was made president of the Scottish Liberal Federation. In 1908 he was created a baronet, no doubt for his services to the party. Four years later Sir Thomas Borthwick was named in the Birthday Honours list as a baron.

On the 20th July 1912 he attended a Boy Scout rally at Potton House with his friend Lord Rosebery. This was his first public appearance after the great honour came to him. It was also his last. He died eleven days later, before the patent of his peerage had passed the Great Seal. So he never assumed the title he had chosen—Baron Whitburgh, of Whitburgh, in the county of Midlothian.

Messages of sympathy came to Lady Borthwick from King George V (this was carried by the Master of Elibank, who was a pall-bearer at the funeral), the then Prime Minister, Asquith, and the Chancellor of the Exchequer, Lloyd George, who had been a guest at Whitburgh the previous autumn. *The Scotsman* published a long obituary, recalling Sir Thomas's political work, his many public appointments and many private acts of generosity, and describing him as 'a plain man, blunt of speech, but with a great gift of commonsense'. The Master of Elibank wrote: 'I have lost a dear friend, the Liberals of Midlothian their leader, and Scotland not only one of her most devoted sons, but also one who, alike in business aptitude and in strength of character, proved himself one of her most typical sons.'

In Whitburgh House a public funeral service was conducted by the minister of Regent Square Presbyterian church, London, of which Sir Thomas had been a faithful member, and a private service by the parish minister of Humbie, the church which he had been used to attend when at Whitburgh.

As the coffin was carried through hamlets and villages where Sir Thomas had been so well known and respected, and along the beautiful Humbie glen, a rainbow spanned the sky: but the ceremony in Humbie churchyard was brightened by a spell of sunshine. He was laid to rest under a great elm, within sound of the burn.

He who leads

The Whitburgh peerage

Sir Thomas's death half-way (so to speak) to a peerage left an unusual situation, though it was not unique. The eldest son, Thomas Banks Borthwick, who of course succeeded to the baronetcy on his father's death, was created Baron Whitburgh a few months later, but with the proviso: 'In remainder to baronetcy only.' That is, the baronetcy, but not the barony, passes to his heir. *Burke's Peerage* further records that 'His Majesty King George V was graciously pleased to ordain and declare . . . that Dame Letitia Mary Borthwick should enjoy the same style and title as if her husband . . . had survived to hold the title and dignity of Baron Whitburgh, but without conferring on her any of the rights or privileges or the precedence belonging by statute or common law to the widow of a Peer of these realms'; and that all the younger children 'should have, hold and enjoy the same title, place, and precedence as if their father had survived to hold the title and dignity of a Baron of the United Kingdom'. Henceforth James, William and Algernon Borthwick and their three sisters were entitled to the prefix 'the Honourable'.

The motto on the Whitburgh Coat of Arms is:

QUI CONDUCIT
He who leads

Some Statistical Notes

Thames Cold Storage Co. Ltd. was formed in 1901 with an issued capital of £60,007 (held by the family, not by the firm) to take over from the partnership Kennet Wharf Cold Store, Upper Thames Street, which had been leased in 1900 for thirty-five years from a company which later became the Union Cold Storage Co. Ltd. (Vesteys): the store is still part of the Union group today. This appears to be the family's first venture in forming a limited company. Later, in 1922, the company was wound up and the lease was transferred to Thomas Borthwick & Sons Ltd. who operated the cold store until the lease expired.

Lancashire Cold Storage Co. Ltd. was formed in 1907 to run the Liverpool cold store, leased from the Lancashire and Yorkshire Railway Company. (In 1962 a new lease was negotiated with their successors, British Railways.) The issued capital was only £504, all held by the family; the company was not wound up until 1932, when the business was transferred to Thomas Borthwick & Sons Ltd.

Smithfield Stalls were acquired from time to time; prices paid to the sitting tenant varied with the location of the stall and the supply and demand position at the time of sale. Stalls could be expensive: £25,000, for example, was paid for 367 shop in 1905—a very large sum of money in those days. Compare this with £19,000 and £16,000 respectively paid in 1933 and 1935 for 89 shop and 264 shop. Smithfield leases are somewhat insubstantial, being under an agreement with the Corporation of London on a weekly basis. These terms of tenure make it prudent to write off the purchase price immediately and Borthwicks place a total book value of £100 on their stalls. Numbers 367, 68 and 16 shops which were all bought before the first world war are still amongst those held by the firm today.

Smithfield porter

CHAPTER SIX

First World War and After

Throughout the first world war Lord Whitburgh alone of the brothers was in charge of the firm in Britain. James Borthwick was resident in New Zealand, paying frequent visits to Australia. Algernon, who had been spending most of his early business life in Australia and New Zealand, came back to England in 1913, served in the Grenadier Guards, and was wounded.

William, readers will remember, had already ceased to take a regular active part in the business, though still a director. He was called to the Bar shortly after the outbreak of war, with every intention of entering politics. He joined the Inns of Court Regiment, served with the King's Royal Rifle Corps, and was seriously wounded and taken prisoner in 1918. He was not sufficiently recovered to lead an active life until 1926, when he first unsuccessfully stood as Liberal candidate for North Dorset. By then he felt he was too old to start a new career as a barrister or, in fact, to take the possibilities of a political career very seriously. The end of the story might have been different if he had followed his bent from the first.

While he was with the firm he had played as big a part in its progress as any of the brothers. His two sons are directors of Borthwicks today; though it is interesting to note that the younger, Brian, had his career interrupted in much the same way as his father. He was at Cambridge when the second world war started, joined the R.N.V.R. immediately, and served on

Atlantic convoys and in escort vessels. After it was over he studied accountancy, joined the firm, and made one trip to Australia and New Zealand.
Then he retired from any regular part in the business to farm his own
property. He is a part-time director.

In 1914 many of the staff of course joined up. Among them was William
Miles, the young clerk whose description of life in the London office has
been quoted. He had an experience now which he remembers more vividly
than any.

In August 1914—the first month of the war—he went off with two pals
to the recruiting office and signed on with the London Regiment. Then he
went to Audrey House, rather wondering how his action would be taken,
and told the secretary. Twist said: 'Very good, William. I am very pleased.
You are not going yet?' He answered: 'No, I have to report at six tonight.'

Within half an hour he was summoned to the directors' room, where
Lord Whitburgh was sitting with Mr James and Mr Algernon. (James was
on one of his visits from New Zealand: Algernon had not yet joined his
regiment.) Lord Whitburgh stood up. 'William,' he said, 'I am very pleased
with what you have done. I wish you the best of luck, and I shall see that
you do not suffer by doing this.' And he shook hands.

'That handshake,' says Miles, 'made all the difference to me. It meant
everything. And, what is more, the firm paid me half salary right through
the war. Perhaps in these days that sort of thing might seem commonplace.
It was not so then.'

The difficulties that had to be faced during the war years were those that
are to be expected at such a time—shortage of staff; the necessity of employing
and training inexperienced men too old or unfit for active service; shortage
of ships; how to get enough supplies through to feed the Forces and civilians
in face of the darkening menace of the U-boats. On the other hand there
were no marketing problems. Except for some by-products normal trading
ceased. Rationing was in force. The Imperial Government Supplies Department took over and all meat and wool were handled under bulk arrangements. Borthwicks continued to tender for Service contracts; and this work
of course became far more important and exacting than in peace time.

At the supplying end

In Australia and New Zealand, James Borthwick and his supporters had
plenty of problems to cope with in getting enough livestock and pushing the

freezing works to their limit. Killing seasons were extended—which meant that beasts were not at their best when killed; but needs must when the devil drives.

To add to the trials, Australia produced one of its periodical dry spells between 1914 and 1916. At first this brought increased offerings to buyers because the farmer, as sensitive to weather prospects as a stockbroker to the market, was anxious to reduce his livestock: Brooklyn killed its first beef in 1914 and built a beef house and a big new brick freezer for the purpose. Then, of course, supplies fell off: Moreton was shut down for about nine months and Portland too experienced a slump. Apart from this it was a matter of killing as many beasts as could be got with staff depleted (although butchers were officially exempt from military service). One Brooklyn butcher, working solo of course, dealt with a hundred sheep on a Saturday morning.

The New Zealand end of the firm received its first notice of a big shake-up in August 1914—a cable from London asking how soon Paki Paki could be started up. This in the middle of the New Zealand winter when all works were closed down and the freezers had been thawed out with braziers. Ted Norman (this was a month or two before he joined up) asked George Croll, the firm's superintending engineer, who said it would take two months. Norman went to see Croll, gave him a good dinner and a few drinks. Croll thawed: he agreed to make it a month. Norman cabled London, whose answer was another question: 'How soon can you start buying stock?' It was pointed out that prices would be high because farmers would not want to sell sheep when they were in wool. London's instructions were: 'Buy all you can.' Paki Paki was the first works in New Zealand killing that season.

Meanwhile Waitara, which had been completely rebuilt in 1904 after the fire, now embarked on a big programme of extensions affecting the slaughter-house, storage and freezing rooms, and the fellmongery, tallow and manure departments. Construction of Belfast, in the South Island, was pressed ahead. It went into operation in December 1916.

Meat companies in general, both in Australia and New Zealand, rose to the occasion and made great efforts; a number of new companies were formed; though naturally everything was chaotic—and a lot of money was made—until the whole business of meat supply was brought under government control. Many new freezing works were put up, primarily to provide extra storage in the event of shipping space not being available at the right time. Various war-time expedients for meat preservation were resorted to, though not on the same scale as in 1939–45. There was a big increase in canning, particularly for the Forces. A canning plant was put up at Moreton, for instance, complete with machinery for making cans from tinplate supplied in sheets. It was closed after the war.

Tribute must be paid to the work done by all the firm's staff in Australia and New Zealand throughout the war, and especially to the two general managers—James Balderstone in Australia, Cuthbert Harper in New Zealand. Harper died a few years later. Balderstone's term of service covered no less than thirty-four years and included both world wars. The part he played in this story cannot be valued adequately.

Ted Norman, the young man who went out from England in 1913 and himself became general manager in New Zealand in due time, was among those who served in the New Zealand forces during the war. He won an M.C. at Gallipoli. Besides his other qualities he was a formidable boxer. Soon after his arrival in the country he went in for the New Zealand amateur middleweight championship and reached the final. He did not win it, however; and there is a story that when he came into the office the next day his appearance was such that he was urged to give up the sport.

After the war

Clerks returning from war service found the London office very much as they had left it—the same high stools and sloping desks, the same wall telephones, the same open fires, the same Pickwickian country department manager regaling himself with pinches of snuff. But they had to accustom themselves to war-time methods of working; for control remained in force until 1921. In 1919 office space at Audrey House was increased by taking on the first floor. The general office remained downstairs.

That year there was another change—a tragic change, and one which affected the clerks particularly, though it was felt also by the directors and by everyone who had to do with head office. Twist, the secretary, was going off for his summer holiday. During the Friday pay-out before he left, William Miles—greatly daring, and listened to with awe by the other clerks—ventured to wish him a good time. He answered: 'Thank you. I'm going to Padstow. I'm told the bathing there is dangerous, so I shall have to be careful.' He spoke half jokingly, for he was a very strong swimmer.

He never came back. He went to help his son, who got into difficulties in the water, and was drowned.

His successor, S. E. H. Savage, was already well known to many at Audrey House, for up to this time he had been with Wederell, Trenow & Gillat, and had been responsible for Borthwicks' audit for many years: it is believed that he worked on it as far back as 1900 when he was an articled clerk. (In the firm's archives is a stout volume bound in red leather, with lock and key—the very first ledger of T. B. & S. (Australasia), dated 1905—which is opened in Savage's handwriting.) A chartered accountant, quiet in manner, neat and dapper in his dress, and extremely thorough, he soon got to know everything about the job. It was not long before he started a re-organization of the office, dividing it into separate departments, each with a head responsible to himself. The tall sloping desks disappeared except a few that remained in the book-keeping department. Savage was secretary until 1952. He was one of the best administrators the firm ever had.

Another addition to the staff occurred within a few months: a new office boy. His name was Joseph Curley. As soon as he reached school-leaving age —fourteen in those days—he set out to look for a job. His father advised him to go into the meat trade. It was not hard to find work when so many men were not yet back from the Services. Two meat companies offered him £1 a week. Mr Savage said he would pay him 17s. 6d. with an extra half-crown after a month's probation. He doesn't know what influenced him except that he liked the look of Borthwicks best and his father advised him to accept their offer.

He was an ambitious boy, restless, and probably a bit of a nuisance to his superiors. After about a year at the post desk he got himself moved to a department, then to another department, then to one of the Smithfield stalls as assistant offal salesman. He was still only eighteen but he was learning all the time. Today he is a director of Borthwicks. There are four directors in London who are not members of the family. Two of them started with the firm as office boys.

In Liverpool immediately after the war (in fact the work was probably started as a war-time measure at the request of the Ministry of Food, with whom there was an agreement about it) the Lancashire Cold Store was substantially enlarged. It was to be extended once again before the second world war.

In Australia and New Zealand the great problem, so long as control remained in force, was still to get enough livestock for the firm's six works and for all the 'outside' works with which it had killing arrangements. The buyers were now mechanised: the senior men had motor-cars and the rest motor bicycles. One difficult area of New Zealand was around Hicks Bay, out on the promontory between Hawkes Bay and the Bay of Plenty. There was a works there that was willing to kill for Borthwicks if it could be supplied with stock. Ted Norman—now back from service in the New Zealand Artillery and appointed second-in-command to Harper—set off with Walter Hill, buyer at Wairoa, to find an agent in Hicks Bay who would buy for the firm. Between Tolaga Bay and Tokomaru Bay, about 20 miles, there was no road: they drove along the beach. There was no bridge over the Waiapu river: they got a Maori boatman to ferry them across. Arriving at Hicks Bay, they found the intended agent too drunk for business. Returning after breakfast in the morning, they fixed the deal. He bought a few lambs; and then the Hicks Bay works closed down. Such was life in New Zealand just after the first world war.

Trends in the trade

As might be expected, Britain's meat imports—which had been increasing steadily through the early years of the century—slumped during the war from 720,000 tons in 1913 to 527,000 in 1919. This decline affected all sources, except that supplies from North America jumped from virtually nil to a peak of 208,000 tons in 1918: this, however, was a flash in the pan. Imports from Australia and New Zealand dropped by more than half. After the war there was a rapid return to pre-war figures and better. Total imports in 1920 were 810,000 tons, including 356,000 from Australia and New Zealand and 434,000 from South America. Britain's home production remained remarkably steady before, during and after the war at a little over a million tons a year.

For those interested, some figures of imports into Britain and meat consumption over the period of our story are given on the next page.

United Kingdom meat consumption over fifty years

1. Please read this chart with caution: it is collated from different sources and 'like' is not compared with 'like' throughout. Where figures are missing, they are not available to us.
2. Up to 1924, the meat figures are taken from the famous Weddel charts, the help of which we gratefully acknowledge, and these relate to mutton, lamb and beef *only*. After this date the figures relate to *all* meats.

3. The figures for total imports include small quantities from other countries than those specified.

4. Home produced meat includes production from imported livestock.

5. The apparent random choice of years is because the information is more readily available for those years, or because it is a year just before or after a war. Despite this somewhat haphazard approach, the trends appear undistorted and an interesting bird's eye picture of 50 years of meat consumption emerges.

	1904	1911	1913	1920	1924	1930	1938	1946	1950	1955	1961
MEAT SUPPLIES (THOUSANDS OF TONS)											
IMPORTED											
North America	120·5	8·9	0·4	18·6	7·9		3·7	131·8	0·2	6·5	18·3
South America	154·9	407·4	447·5	434·5	654·3	633·2	515·7	323·0	301·8	234·5	211·1
Australia	12·8	100·1	150·7	154·7	60·2	81·5	232·1	107·6	130·9	179·9	69·2
New Zealand	90·1	112·0	122·2	197·3	148·4	187·1	271·3	311·9	347·9	325·2	319·0
TOTAL IMPORTS	378·3	628·4	720·8	810·4	875·7	937·6	1058·6	938·7	810·1	804·8	733·6
HOME PRODUCED	1287·8	1192·3	1105·4	1042·1	1107·9	1011·0	1088·3	831·8	944·0	1373·2	1752·6
TOTAL AVAILABLE U.K.	1666·1	1820·7	1826·2	1852·5	1983·6	1948·6	2146·9	1770·5	1754·1	2178·0	2486·2
Percentage of Home Produced to Total	77·5	65·5	60·5	56·3	55·9	51·9	50·7	47·0	53·8	63·1	70·5
U.K. population (millions)	40·0	42·1	42·3	44·0	45·0	46·0	47·5	49·2	50·0	51·0	52·8
ESTIMATED ANNUAL CONSUMPTION (LBS. PER HEAD)											
Meat	93·3	96·9	96·8	94·3	98·7	94·9	98·1	76·8	82·6	96·9	103·5
Associated produce:											
Poultry							5·1*		5·6†	6·4	14·6
Canned Meat: Domestic							1·4*				2·6
Imported				2·5	2·5		3·1	13·7	8·5	8·5	8·8
Bacon and Ham				15·1‡	23·7‡		28·1*	18·1	21·4	25·8	26·3

* Pre-war Average   † 1951   ‡ Imported

CHAPTER SEVEN

Eighteen Years in Britain

In 1921 came the end of war-time controls and a return to normal free enterprise working of the meat trade. James Borthwick had come home from New Zealand in 1920. For the next twenty years and more the firm's affairs in Britain were in the hands of the three brothers—Lord Whitburgh, James and Algernon. None of them went to Australia or New Zealand again. This strenuous part of the management job was now delegated to the next generation. Algernon's two sons, Algy and Pat, were in both countries pretty frequently from 1928 onwards. In 1929 Pat made his home in New Zealand. He married a descendant of one of the country's oldest pioneer families.

It is noticeable that there was a gap of eight years when none of the family visited either Australia or New Zealand. This is exceptional: nothing like it happened before or since. The apparent inaction that descended on the three brothers contrasts with their father's sense of mission and his whole philosophy; it seems to confirm what social historians have often remarked—that the spirit which drove Victorian merchants waned in the inter-war years. But it is worth while to examine their motives, or lack of motives, in more detail. Is what the social historians say true in this case? And, if it is, can we find any cause?

To begin with, each brother had personal reasons for staying at home. A

big part of Lord Whitburgh's interest was always in farming and his Midlothian estate. Algernon's health was not good: it was very bad from 1929
onwards. James had the best reason—that he had only just returned from a
long spell in New Zealand and it was someone else's turn. But apart from
these there were two considerations of a more general nature which carried
much greater weight. The first was concerned with that sinister figure whose
growing shadow falls on all sorts of commercial developments—the tax
inspector.

As long ago as 1905 tax considerations had had a bearing on the decision
to start T. B. & S. (Australasia); though the rates then in force now seem
negligible. During the first world war they began to increase; and so in
particular did what was then called super-tax—a special tax on those
wealthy people (they were wealthy in those days) with incomes over
£2,000 a year. Tax avoidance—any legitimate device to escape tax, as
distinct from tax evasion, which is not legitimate—had not then become a
major industry; but it was attracting attention. Some super-tax payers
spotted that they could do themselves good by converting their estates into
companies. There was no super-tax on the income of companies but only
on the dividends they paid out. These tax avoidance companies paid out
in dividends only as much as their shareholders needed to spend: the rest
they left to accumulate, paying no super-tax on it.

The tax authorities were wise to this dodge before long. It was dealt with
in the Finance Act of 1921, whose famous Section 22 gave the Special Com-
missioners power, if a company that could pay dividends did not do so, or
even if it failed to pay out a reasonable proportion of its profits as dividends,
to direct that the whole of that company's profits should be treated as
dividends and taxed accordingly. No indication was given of what was a
'reasonable proportion'.

There is no reason to suppose that this measure had any sinister purpose,
nor that it was aimed at *bona fide* businesses. It has certainly never been
invoked against Borthwicks. But, at the time, the directors took the view
that it was going to bear heavily on them. They thought it was an attack
on private companies as such. It was in fact, as it now appears, really an
attack on bogus companies that were not really traders: but one trouble
with tax legislation is that nets to catch sharp practice men sometimes
penalise honest businesses.

The meat trade has its ups and downs, and a firm like Borthwicks must
build up reserves in good times to tide over bad times. The directors thought

that Section 22 would prevent them from doing this, and also that it would prevent them from saving up the money needed for expansion. (It has always been Borthwicks' pride that their organisation on both sides of the world was built up by ploughing back money that had been *earned*.) Events have proved that they were mistaken on both counts. But the thought was in their minds; and it affected the firm's progress for a good many years afterwards.

Other things happened about the same time and together, like straws in the wind, influenced the directors' thinking in much the same direction. These occurred on the other side of the world and so are reserved for the next chapter. Now it is time to follow developments in Britain; which—though there were plenty of difficulties and emergencies—went ahead at a good pace.

Lord Whitburgh was in charge of marketing. He had his father's business ability but, according to the times, was more flexible in his outlook. Old Sir Thomas, for instance, would never allow an employee to bring a newspaper to work. He would say: 'I don't pay you to follow the racing results. Your job is to sell meat.' Lord Whitburgh, on the other hand, when a question of working hours arose, would say: 'I don't care what hours you work so long as you do your job.' He was courteous and considerate always. If any of his staff was at all unwell, he would notice it. To one who worked closely with him, whenever he thought he was not looking up to the mark, he recommended a course of halibut liver pills.

Expansion and adaptation continued. Between the two world wars Borthwicks opened depots in fifteen more provincial towns in England, Scotland and Wales, some with their own small cold stores attached, and acquired five more stalls in the Central Markets at Smithfield. It was during the early twenties that Bristol was developed into an important branch, with sub-branches at Bath, Cheltenham and Weston-super-Mare, supplying the whole of the West of England, and its direct road delivery service from Avonmouth was started.

The firm's retail business, run by a subsidiary under the name of John English & Company, was finally closed down in 1921. Borthwicks have never regretted their decision to stick henceforth to the 'wholesale only' rule in Britain. It was closely linked with all the developments in service to the butchers, and was certainly popular with them. Some publicity was given to it a few years later in the form of a statement printed on the weekly price lists issued to country customers, and this was followed by a noticeable increase in turnover which continued steadily.

The distributive organisation had, as it has now, two main focal points: one, the cold stores, where orders were taken by telephone during the night and the meat was cut up and loaded on to vans for delivery to shops before opening time; the other, the markets—not only at Smithfield, Liverpool and Manchester, but also in other large towns such as Glasgow and Birmingham —where the firm had stalls. At all these places the job demanded working at peculiar hours. This the staff accepted cheerfully, though it entailed some inconvenience and sacrifice. Joe Curley—who was working his way up from office boy to director and got himself moved to Smithfield in 1924—used to leave Hornsey, where he was living, at eight minutes past three every morning by steam train for King's Cross, where he took a taxi to the market, arriving about 4 a.m., and finishing at 1 p.m. 'The great snag in working those hours,' he says, 'was the difficulty of keeping in touch with other young men. One got cut off from old friends. But of course one made new ones.'

The firm's Smithfield operations at this time were in charge of R. G. Bremner, who had succeeded Bob Wilson. Born at Thurso in the north of Scotland, Bremner started his business life with Eastmans, the Glasgow butchers, and later joined the firm of Gordon Woodroffe, who dealt as agents in various imported products including meat. This brought him into touch with Borthwicks. It is said that he once bought some lambs from them at 5d. a pound and sold them back two hours later at $5\frac{1}{2}d$. At all events Borthwicks were sufficiently impressed to offer him a job, which he accepted, as super-intendent of their Smithfield stalls. This was in 1923. For the next sixteen years he worked very closely with Lord Whitburgh—a relationship which he himself describes as 'Boswell to Lord Whitburgh's Johnson'. It was he who was advised to take halibut liver pills. Whether he ever took them he does not relate: but he has happily survived a long and strenuous working life, including thirty-six years with Borthwicks—twenty-one of them as a director —during which he gave outstanding service to the firm and to the meat trade. In time Joe Curley became his assistant.

In 1923—the same year as Bremner joined—the firm took on another office boy who was destined to become a director. This was Alec Fyffe. Though the start and the summit of his career were the same as Curley's, the route he took was different. He began at Kennet Wharf. After this he came to Audrey House, where he worked for some years in various depart-ments. Then he was put on to keeping certain statistics for the directors. In this work he showed a notable talent, with the result that he was soon assisting R. G. Bremner on the statistical side of meat marketing. Except during the second world war—he was a prisoner in Japanese hands for four years—statistics and costing have been his particular province. He was appointed a director in 1959.

The story of a successful business is usually, in part at least, a story of developing organisation. This word 'organisation' creates a faint uneasiness. One feels that things are settling into an efficient, safe, dull routine which nothing can disturb. In fact this never happens. Always something crops up —some emergency that disrupts, demanding fresh initiative and improvisation. An instance came now in the general strike of May 1926.

Faced with the prospect of a breakdown in the machinery of distribution, Borthwicks called for volunteers to work at Kennet Wharf. Quite a number of the office staff came forward. They were there about a fortnight, loading meat from the cold store on to lorries and railway vans. After eight hours of this they had had enough and used to drop off to sleep. There was no question of getting home, so the firm arranged supplies of bedding and a canteen. At night they played cards and darts.

One difficulty was beer. Some of the men, who would not go out because of the pickets, persuaded Joe Curley, the youngster of the party, to fetch some for them from the local pub. He got there safe enough, but on the way back with his pockets full of bottles the pickets grabbed him. They pinched the beer and gave him what he describes as 'a bit of a shaking up'. He returned to the cold store pretty scared and, what was worse, with no beer.

One of the measures which the firm took to meet the strike was the starting of a road delivery service centred on Bristol, like that which was already operating from London. It was intended as a temporary expedient, but was such a success with butchers and dealers that it was made permanent, replacing the old rail service throughout the West of England, and reaching as far as Penzance. This is regarded as one of the landmarks in the history of the Bristol branch between the wars. Though it probably would have come some time anyway, it was in fact born of the strike: an instance of the old saying that 'it's an ill wind that blows nobody any good'.

At the end of 1927 Thomas Borthwick & Sons Limited was wound up. This is not the end of the story. A new company of the same name was formed immediately; and this is the company that is in being today. The decision to go into voluntary liquidation stemmed largely from two causes. The Finance Act of 1921 was one of them. The other—to be described in greater detail later on—was that certain developments had occurred in New Zealand which made the directors think that Borthwicks' New Zealand business would be substantially curtailed and that, even if this were not the case, there would be no possibilities for further expansion. In this belief they were proved wrong by future events (although one or two things happened immediately which appeared to confirm their belief). However, business decisions spring not from hind-thought but from attempted fore-thought; and what matters here is not what actually happened later but what the directors thought was likely to happen.

In the view which the directors took at the time, here was a company with respectable resources built up out of earnings, but a company whose business in Australia and New Zealand would be prevented by Government action from further development and, indeed, would probably have to be curtailed, and a company in which further expansion would be impossible because it would not be permitted to accumulate the money required. In sum, they considered that the Finance Act of 1921 plus the threat of restrictions to be described later would mean that the business could not grow beyond its present size and indeed would probably have to contract.

In these circumstances they decided—quite reasonably on the face of it—to take out those reserves which would not be needed for what they imagined would be a smaller business, and to form a new company with capital more in line with the resources that would actually be required. The old company had a capital of £300,000 with large reserves: the new company had a capital of £1,650,000 with no reserves. In other words, £1,350,000 of reserves were capitalised and the rest was distributed to the shareholders.

In the light of later events the correctness of the decision must at times have appeared doubtful because of the slump which lasted from 1929 to 1932; but after that the new company made satisfactory profits and by 1939 its revenue reserves were nearly £1 million.

This is the place, though not strictly in order of date, to record two events that happened a few years later. In 1933 another Borthwick came into the firm. This was Jason, son of William and cousin of Algy and Pat. He had studied law at Cambridge and was called to the Bar in the same year as he joined Borthwicks. A few years after—following what was almost a family tradition by this time—he married a New Zealand girl, Miss Elizabeth Elworthy, of Timaru.

The same year, 1933, Wederell, Trenow & Gillat, the auditors who had helped to put the original limited company on its feet and had kept those feet on the straight and narrow path of accountancy ever since, retired from the scene. Their responsibilities, now very much greater, were taken over by Deloitte, Plender, Griffiths & Company. This distinguished firm, needless to say, carried on the good work. It is doing so still.

The cold stores

The first major developments which the new company undertook in Britain were concerned with its cold stores. The lease of Kennet Wharf expired in 1934. By that time, however, a brand new cold store was built and ready for action. For a description of this huge building—a landmark on the river and, of course, a focal point in the firm's operations today—we cannot do better than quote from the illustrated booklet which was issued to celebrate its opening:

> Designed by Sir Edwin Cooper, A.R.A., it has a commanding ultra-modern appearance. What is more practical and important, however, is that it is fitted with every up-to-date appliance and device to give efficient storage powers and adequate means of speedy collection and despatch of goods. The full storage capacity is approximately 300,000 carcases.
>
> . . . the equipment includes three compressors, any two of which, when working together, are capable of maintaining a temperature of 16 degrees Fahr., even during the hottest summer days. The chambers are cooled by the direct expansion system, and the amount of piping used in this system would, if placed end to end, stretch for a distance of 22 miles. All the hoists and lifts are electrically driven for conveying the produce to the many floors and chambers. No expense has, indeed, been withheld in order to make this Store among the best in this country.
>
> The choice of site at Deptford was made so that good road and river approaches were available to give ready and speedy access to the building. This will speed up deliveries, for with a 185 ft. frontage, free from building supports, 14 lorries can enter and be loaded at the same time.
>
> Another outstanding feature of the new building is the huge canopy which juts out over the river side, to the extent of 40 feet, where the river craft unload. This allows four insulated barges (each 90 ft. by 22 ft.) to berth alongside and be discharged under cover, thus giving protection

to the produce against adverse weather conditions. Eight barges of the above dimensions will be able to berth and be discharged on the one tide.

With regard to 'ultra-modern appearance', we must remember that this phrase meant something different in the thirties from what it means in the sixties. Whether the change is for the better is a matter of opinion. As to expense—here again ideas have changed in thirty years. A figure of £250,000 seems very little in relation to the size of the building and what it contains. Today it could hardly be less than £1 million. A good investment made at the right time.

The address (appropriately) was Butcher Row, Deptford, though the name has since been changed to Borthwick Street. The building was named Borthwick Wharf.

There were developments in Liverpool also about this time. In 1931 the meat market—'the Smithfield of Liverpool'—was moved from the place where it had been since 1912 to a new building that had been constructed for it. This is called Stanley Meat Market. It occupies the site of the old Stanley Cattle Market; and Borthwicks' stall is on the exact spot where, nearly ninety years ago, Thomas Borthwick used to stand in his silk hat, selling live cattle to butchers and dealers. One might wonder whether any part of him still haunts the place; what he thinks of the electric band-saws that cut up a carcase in a few quick passes; and whether he communicates anything to those busy white-coated men as they go about his firm's affairs.

Certainly they remember him. Nowhere will you hear so many stories of him. And nowhere is the firm's family spirit more noticeable than in this market, in the Liverpool office, and the Lancashire Cold Store. The men here have an unbeaten record of faithfulness to the firm. Twelve who retired between 1957 and 1960 had worked for Borthwicks for a total of 577 years; and six of them had received the gold watch that the directors give in recognition of fifty years' service. This list does not include H. Jasper, assistant chamber foreman in the cold store, who joined in 1914. In his eightieth year he was still doing a good job in the chambers—in a temperature of 16 degrees Fahrenheit—and did not want to retire.

The Lancashire Cold Store was enlarged again a few years later, in 1936. The top four of its eight floors were extended, bringing its total capacity up to some 3,500 tons. The carcases and quarters that lie in its great icy chambers have come direct from the works in Australia and New Zealand to Liverpool port. They will go out again to Stanley Market some six miles away, to the markets in Manchester and Leeds, or to 'country delivery' areas from Cumberland to Staffordshire and North Wales.

Among the twenty-six insulated vans that are garaged here is one larger than the rest: an articulated vehicle consisting of haulage unit (engine and cab) with detachable trailer. It came from London last night and will start the return journey this evening. Exactly halfway—at Meriden, in Warwickshire—it will meet its fellow. There will be a quick change of trailers so that the drivers with their cabs can each return to his own home, and the two vans will go on through the darkness. This nightly shuttle service enables the two great centres to co-operate in a quick adjustment of supply to demand. There are few nights when both vans are not heavily laden.

One further event to record before once more we turn the clock back and begin to live through the same years on the other side of the world. John Borthwick, son of James, born in Melbourne near the end of the first world war, came into the firm just before the outbreak of the second. He started in March 1939, as a junior salesman at Smithfield—a rich new beginning to his education after Eton. But in any case it must have been difficult to settle down. The clouds of war were gathering; and the meat traders of Britain, with a foresight which might with advantage have commended itself to the politicians, had been for some time preparing themselves to meet a possible emergency. It was only a matter of months before this young man, like a million others, was in uniform.

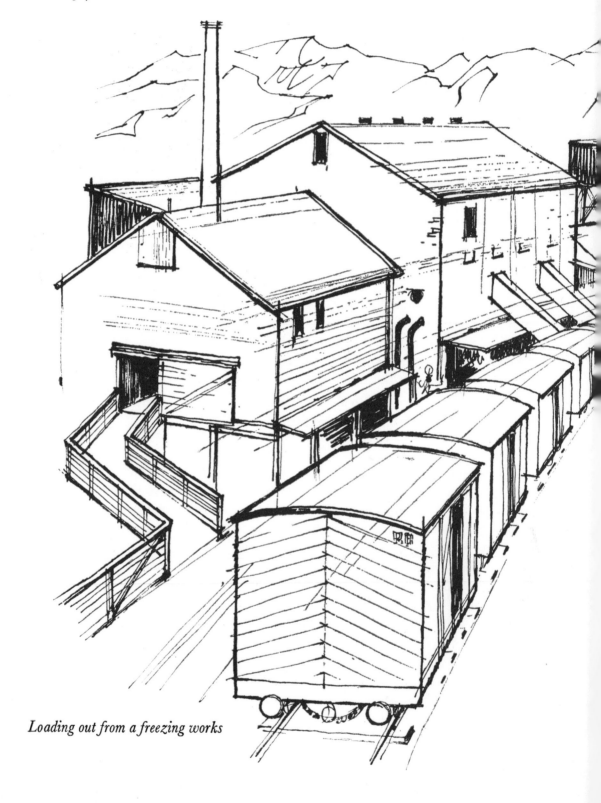

Loading out from a freezing works

CHAPTER EIGHT

Eighteen Years in the Southern Hemisphere

At the end of the first world war there were big stocks of meat in store in Australia and New Zealand as well as in Britain. Until these were liquidated they blocked the smooth flow of supplies all along the line from the works back to the cattle and sheep stations. Prices were at a low level; and the situation was not improved by the world slump that followed the post-war boom, nor by the continuation of controls until 1921. The New Zealand farmers' troubles led to the formation, in 1922, of the New Zealand Meat Producers' Board, which since then has supervised the grading of meat for export, regulated shipments, and done good work in advertising New Zealand meat in overseas markets.

This was one of those straws in the wind, referred to in the previous chapter, which at the time influenced the Borthwick directors against all-out expansion in Australia and New Zealand. They felt that the Board—which represented the farmers and had complete power of control—could grow into an instrument of discrimination against 'overseas' companies. (It is necessary here to explain the significance of the word 'overseas'—this for the benefit of those U.K. readers who may think it is merely a geographical expression. If a visitor goes to New Zealand from the United Kingdom, he is certain of a warm welcome. New Zealanders have been described as more British than the British, and even New Zealanders of several generations' standing refer to Britain as the 'old country' or 'home'; but if a New Zealander or a New Zealand company wishes to arouse prejudice against British capital or a British concern he does not describe them as British. He describes them as 'overseas', or even 'foreign'. A similarly interesting example of the use of words happens in Britain. If a New Zealand rugby football team comes to England they will be assured of a warm welcome, in spite of their tiresome habit of always winning! But if a member of the English National Farmers' Union wishes to protest about New Zealand lamb or butter, he does not use the word New Zealand but either 'imported' or 'foreign'. So much for etymology.)

The view that Borthwicks took of the potential powers of the Board and its probable actions was apparently confirmed within a few years by various moves on the part of the New Zealand Government which will be referred to. They also thought that Australia was going to follow the same path.

Events proved them quite wrong about Australia and roughly 50 per cent wrong about New Zealand. But this was what they thought, not entirely without reason: and the view they took on this question—as on the probable effects of the 1921 Finance Act—materially influenced their decisions.

It was about this time, incidentally, that the 'open door' policy was introduced in New Zealand's meat trade. This requires any works, Borthwicks included, to kill stock for farmers on request, charging the appropriate rate and handing back the meat after processing. It gives any farmer who thinks that the meat companies are not offering him good enough prices, or that he can make a better profit by selling his own meat, the opportunity to export on his own account. It is still in force.

When conditions returned to normal the trade in general resumed its advance. Britain's meat imports from all sources (excluding such 'extras' as pork and poultry), which amounted to some 810,000 tons in 1920—even then substantially more than before the war—exceeded a million tons in 1938. South America still held the lion's share of this business (two-thirds of the total in 1930, which was not exceptional) while supplies from Australia and New Zealand declined gradually, until the Ottawa agreement of 1932 brought in a system of preferences which were of enormous benefit to the Commonwealth countries. To say that Australia's exports to Britain were more than doubled in eight years would be misleading, for they have always been rather irregular owing largely to periodical droughts. New Zealand's, which keep a steadier course, went up by nearly 30 per cent in the same time.

The boom of post-war years was followed in the autumn of 1929 by an almost world-wide slump. Triggered off by over-speculation on the New York and London Stock Exchanges, it led to the liquidation of many companies and the ruin of individuals. By way of illustration, in England during 1929 no less than 36 new companies whose prospectuses showed estimated profits totalling £3½ million suffered in the event losses of almost £1 million.

The United States Government, attempting to stem the tide, misused their gold stocks and spread the contagion. Collapsing credit caused order books to feel the pinch; trade barriers went up in self-defence, and Governments imposed import restrictions.

The British Government of the day was pledged to Free Trade and so producers always had one market open for meat. Their reaction was the reverse of the industrial slowdown: unemployment was rife in the towns, but the farmer on such occasions merely produces more to safeguard the roof over his head. Furthermore, the reduced demand for wool caused prices to drop to a point where it became more profitable to raise fat lambs.

Percy Allen—one of the firm's senior men in New Zealand: he was a boy in the Waitara works when Borthwicks bought it in 1902, became works manager and later a district manager, and completed fifty years' service before he retired—was on a visit to London at this time. He remembers Lord Whitburgh saying to him that he would like, as a matter of policy, always to pay high enough prices for livestock to allow the farmer to put something back into the land. This was an ideal. In practice no firm can buy stuff without reference to probable realisations; at least they cannot do it for long. The depression was general: it was not even confined to the meat trade. But farmers are human; and when such things happen they naturally tend to blame the meat companies who hand them their cheques. It may not occur to them that no company is in control of economic trends. A world dictator might conceivably iron out all price fluctuations: but he would have to be all-powerful, in control of all supplies *and* all markets.

In Australia

Over the impact of that depression Borthwicks were well able to sympathise with their valued clients the farmers. Being cattle raisers themselves they suffered the same shocks. There is documentary evidence of this in an old file that was kept in the little wooden office behind the Banchory homestead. The correspondence begins with a letter dated the 12th January 1931, from J. S. Balderstone, general manager in Australia and a director of T. B. & S. (Australasia) Limited, 84 William Street, Melbourne, to Mr Ken Goodwin, Banchory Station, Queensland. (Banchory had had several managers since Ted Tooker. Sam Goodwin had been given the job in 1919 and by this time had handed it over to his son Ken. Ken's story is that his father woke him up at two o'clock one morning and said: 'You're taking over the management of Banchory as from now.')

This letter is a masterpiece: a firm statement of unpleasant facts combined with delicate diplomacy. It begins with a reference to the economic and financial situation in the United Kingdom and the need, in everyone's interests, to reduce production costs in Australia. Advices from London are 'anything but cheerful' for the prospects of beef: the prices of by-products either show no change or are declining. Will Mr Goodwin consider his wage rates? He will know best what other stations in his district are doing in this matter; and of course allowance will be made for the responsibilities of married men. His opinion will be valued. Incidentally, though the company is very well pleased with Mr Goodwin's management of Banchory, it may be necessary later to adjust his own position.

There is no copy of Goodwin's reply in the file. But it is quite evident that he said exactly what he was bound to say in answer to such a letter, both as to wage rates and his own position. James Balderstone's next is a grateful acknowledgment of Mr Goodwin's excellent advice, which the company have decided to act on.

That difficult period had repercussions in Queensland which are not entirely forgotten today. The cattlemen—being no less human than the farmers—resented their employers' action. But what could the employers do? Though it must be admitted that some of them probably took the occasion to treat their men more hardly than was absolutely necessary.

Banchory weathered this storm as it weathered others. Ken Goodwin was an excellent manager, a Queenslander through and through, and one of Borthwicks' most faithful supporters. As time went on James Balderstone, a shrewd and cautious general manager, left many more important decisions to him. Among other developments, it was Ken who took the initiative in introducing the first polled shorthorn bulls that were seen in central Queensland. Their influence can easily be seen in the Banchory stock today. It is one of Ken Goodwin's legacies.

Before this time, in 1924, Borthwicks had bought for £A.40,000 the freehold of another property, Thornhill—a fattening station on the coast near Bundaberg, some 250 miles north of Brisbane. This was disposed of for £A.130,000 in 1959 (no vast capital profit, if one bears in mind how money values had changed). Ken Goodwin managed Thornhill for some years after the second world war. Then he became pastoral inspector for all the firm's cattle properties in Queensland. His death in 1962—a fortnight before he was due to retire, having served Borthwicks for forty-three years—was a very great loss.

A glance at the map shows that Brisbane and the Moreton works are very near the southern border of Queensland, and that the railway from Brisbane runs roughly westwards. Some 600 miles farther north, through Charters Towers and Cloncurry, stretches another railway whose stations are the focus of stock routes that serve the northern parts of Queensland and the Northern Territory. Somewhere near the eastern terminus of this railway was the obvious place for Borthwicks' next freezing works. A works at Burdekin, near Charters Towers, came on the market about 1928. Monte Moss, one of the Borthwick men now retired who live around Brisbane (Monte's record of nearly fifty-two years' service to the firm is the longest in Australia), tells how he went up to reconnoitre and sent back his report— a coded telegram more than 200 words long—from Charters Towers. The lease of Burdekin was taken.

The results of the first year's working were excellent. Borthwicks offered good prices which were popular with the farmers. Then the effects of the slump made themselves felt. Burdekin was a very old works and its maintenance costs were heavy. It was given up after two seasons.

It was replaced by another works in northern Queensland—at Merinda, near Bowen, east of Charters Towers and on the coast. Bowen and its port, Port Denison, had been active in the meat export business for half a century by that time. The works at Merinda first went into operation in 1896. When Borthwicks bought it at the end of 1932 its annual kill had grown to just under 20,000 head. Since then it has touched 57,000.

In New Zealand

Cuthbert Harper, the first man officially to hold the title of general manager in New Zealand, died in the year of decontrol, 1921, after eleven years in office. He was succeeded by W. H. E. Flint, who was known in the trade as 'Willie' and who remained general manager for the next ten years.

Borthwicks never went into stock raising in New Zealand as they did in Australia. The story of the firm in New Zealand between the wars is largely a story of the works—two more works added to the list; one existing works wiped off the map by an Act of God; others in peril by fire; extensions and improvements.

Among the companies that flourished during the first world war but got into difficulties after it was the Wairarapa Farmers' Meat Company. This company's works at Waingawa is excellently placed—in the southern part of the North Island, in the middle of prosperous sheep country. It came into the possession of the Bank of New Zealand, who asked Borthwicks if they would take it. Ted Norman (Flint was away in England at the time) cabled the offer to London, who agreed provided the works was in good shape. There was delay because the New Zealand Government refused to let Borthwicks have the licence. The objection was overcome thanks to representations by the bank and the farmers; and Waingawa was bought for £120,000 in time for the 1928-9 killing season.

In the meantime the Government's attitude about the licence helped to confirm the directors' feeling that there was discrimination against 'overseas' companies in New Zealand.

Through Waingawa Borthwicks went into soap manufacture for a time. Attached to the works when they took it over was a concrete building with the words USE EVEREST SOAP in large letters on the roof. The soap factory got its main raw material, fat, from the meat works. It was carried on as such for several years. Now it is the home of the experimental workshops.

It was soon after this, in 1930, that the firm's New Zealand head office was moved to the North Island. Christchurch remained, as it is still, the South Island headquarters, controlling the Belfast works and the buying offices and keeping close relations with the 'outside' works in the South Island.

With three works in the North Island as against one in the South, the move was a logical step. But the choice of site—Masterton, a town in the Wairarapa—was not. Masterton is an agreeable place to live in and to work in; it is near Waingawa and within a day's car journey of both Waitara and Paki Paki. But in other respects, as was evident in time, it was hardly suitable for Borthwicks' New Zealand headquarters. However, for all those who lived and worked there, the years in the Wairarapa are a happy memory.

About this time 'Willie' Flint was called back to England. He left the firm soon afterwards and returned to New Zealand, where he became a director of the New Zealand Refrigerating Company and, later, its chairman. Ted Norman, who was now settled at Masterton, succeeded him as Borthwicks' general manager. He was then forty-three. Pat Borthwick, a young man of twenty-two, also moved to be within reach of the new headquarters. In fact Te Whanga, near Masterton, is his home today. He became a director of the company in 1931.

The 3rd February 1931 is a date that will be long remembered in New Zealand: the date of the great earthquake. In Hawke's Bay it was a typical summer morning. The Paki Paki works had started taking in stock for killing and the slaughter boards were hard at work, when suddenly walls buckled and fell and machines were wrenched from their fixtures. In seconds the buildings were a wreck.

It was lucky that this happened during 'smoke-o' when most of the men were outside enjoying a breather. Rescue operations were quickly in hand. The injured were carried to the lawn behind the office, where all employees were assembled for a check. By 1 p.m., about two hours after the first big shock, all who were badly hurt had been taken to the emergency clearing station at Hastings. One man died there. Three bodies had been found in the rubble. Another man lost a leg: his name was Kelly, and he was afterwards foreman butcher at Waingawa.

The shocks were felt in Masterton about 120 miles away. Pat Borthwick and Ted Norman were there. They had been trying to get in touch with Paki Paki for some time when they heard a radio in the main street calling for doctors and nurses to go to Hawke's Bay. They set off in a car about five o'clock. It was a terrible journey—there were great cracks in the road—and it took six hours. They found one structure standing amid the wreckage. This was the store. It was full of meat and, miraculously, though the freezing machinery was out of action, the insulation was more or less intact.

Could the meat be saved? The chief engineer, Frank Smaill, though black and exhausted like everyone else, came with them to look at it. He thought it would keep for a few days. After making sure that the injured were looked after and all employees accounted for, they got into the car and started back. Reaching Masterton about two in the morning, they stopped for a clean up and something to eat. Then they drove straight on to Wellington to try to arrange for a ship to take on the meat there after it was railed from Paki Paki.

Reaching Wellington early in the morning, they went to the Meat Board to get first call on all insulated trucks in the North Island, then to the

Port Line who at once arranged for a ship to be diverted to Wellington to take on the meat. Everyone helped all they could.

After that Pat Borthwick stayed in Masterton, keeping in touch by motor cycle despatch rider—a job for which one of the firm's men volunteered—while Norman went back to Paki Paki to see the meat put on rail. Trucks were ready and the line was being repaired. But the men were not keen to go into the store: the ground was still shaking suggestively. The foreman said: 'If you come with me they'll follow.' He picked up a hurricane lantern—it was night and of course the electricity was off—and ducked through the 'port', the small square entrance into the store. Norman went after him; and sure enough the men followed.

They worked night and day and got all the meat out. The railway men too did a fine job. Altogether 80,000 'freight carcases'—over 2,000 tons of good meat—were saved and shipped to England. It was all insured, so it was the insurance company that got the benefit of their efforts. But nobody thought about that. Meat was their job.

The policy on the works itself did not cover earthquake risks. It had cost £55,000. A big loss to Borthwicks.

Today at Napier, some 16 miles north of Paki Paki, is a wide expanse of good agricultural land that was the bottom of the inner harbour until the 1931 earthquake lifted it up. On the open shore the sea retreated, adding about 50 yards to the width of dry beach all along the Marine Parade.

And at Paki Paki tall trees that have grown since that day cast their hard, black shadows over broken concrete and weeds where the works once stood. Most of the Paki Paki staff had been moved to Masterton; and there, with the agreement of the Union and various Government departments, stock bought by the firm in Hawke's Bay was killed at night for the rest of that season. It was brought down by rail. So Borthwicks were able to satisfy their clients and to keep their connections in the district.

After the 1931–2 season the Hawke's Bay Farmers' Meat Company agreed to kill for Borthwicks at their Whakatu works, near Hastings. This excellent arrangement is still in force.

But, in spite of it, Borthwicks now needed another works in the southern part of the North Island. For some years the firm had been taking over the whole output of the Feilding Farmers' Freezing Company. After the loss of Paki Paki they bought the Feilding works, which is a few miles from the town of that name, at Aorangi. It lies at the heart of one of the richest sheep farming districts. Its annual kill, though larger than Waingawa's, is made

Merino hoggets are mustered on a high-country block in Canterbury, New Zealand

Belfast Works in 1923–24 showing the solo slaughtermen at their hooks. The two 'Judas' sheep (specially fitted with collars to avoid accidents!) are pets, which lead the sheep up the ramp from the yards to the slaughter pens, but then dodge away into safety

Belfast Works mutton chain today. A description of the operation of the chain is given at the foot of the works 'flow' diagram on pages 128–9

Mustering sheep on a Hawkes Bay station in the North Island of New Zealand

This and the two following pictures form a sequence. When New Zealand lambs are in prime condition, the farmer brings them (usually early in the morning) to the drafting yards

117

The buyer runs the lambs through the race, picking only those that are ready for the works. This is a big day for the farmer and all his family will probably be there to help or watch

After drafting, the fat lambs are loaded on to waiting trucks and go straight off to the works. After resting in the yards for an hour or two, they move up a ramp to be slaughtered — at the rate of one every 6 and a half seconds, so their end is quick, humane and efficient

A country sheep sale at Featherston, in the North Island of New Zealand

up in about the same proportions—a great many sheep and lambs of the finest quality, a lot of beef, some calves and pigs. Though it is a big works its buying area is astonishingly small. So productive is the immediate neighbourhood that Feilding can draw most of its stock from within a radius of 25 miles. Being central, it has rail access to several ports. It uses Wellington mostly; occasionally, like Waitara, it ships through New Plymouth; occasionally through Napier in Hawke's Bay.

Waitara—Borthwicks' first works, rebuilt in 1904, substantially extended at the beginning of the first world war, and subjected to various additions and reconstructions at intervals—started another major extension of all departments in 1937 to cope with an increasing kill.

But if any optimist thought that everything was now on an even keel he soon learnt that earthquake is not the only hazard. To begin with, some time before this, the mouth of the Waitara river was permanently blocked by a sand bar. The works wharf and the lighters went out of use; and since then Waitara's products have been taken by rail to Port Taranaki, the port of New Plymouth. Then, the works had hardly settled down from its latest extensions when fire broke out in the bag factory and spread quickly to the beef slaughterhouse, the beef chiller and mutton cooling room. Effective action prevented a major disaster.

A much more serious fire attacked Waingawa soon after—in February 1939. It started near the wool department and, licking up trestles and roof joists, swept over the chillers to the freezing block. This was a Saturday evening and many of the men were on their way to the pictures in Masterton. When they saw smoke in the distance they dumped their families and jumped on their bikes. 'The road was packed with bikes and cars,' one of them recalls. 'All Masterton and Carterton seemed to be on the way.'

The man who gives this account is L. B. Lee, now a foreman at Feilding. He says nothing of his own exploits that night. But it is known that he, like others, did grand work, especially in guiding firemen over danger-spots on the roofs. He was in such a mess at the end of it that no one could recognise him as the man who a few hours before was peacefully on his way to the cinema. Jim Nelson, foreman butcher at Waingawa (he is still there), put on baseball clothes and with the 'board walker' (his assistant) spent most of the night sorting out a mass of twisted rails that had been the hoisting machinery on the beef slaughter floor.

The Masterton and Carterton fire brigades were early on the scene. With the men's help they saved the freezing block. But the slaughterhouse, cooling room and part of the freezer and fellmongery were wiped out. The chains (chain killing had been installed in all works some years before) were out of action.

All the men reported for work next morning and started clearing up the mess. The Masterton builders came on the job as a team. On the Monday week three chains were working under an improvised lean-to roof. That week they killed 6,000 per day.

Nature still had one card up her sleeve. That winter there was a six-inch fall of snow, which was without precedent in the Wairarapa. But the temporary roof stood up to it.

Off the main stream

While the export of frozen beef, mutton and lamb was at all times by far the greater part of the business, other activities were engaged in. These differ in importance. All add variety and interest to the work.

The possibilities of chilled beef shipment were often in mind: with the example of South America they could not be forgotten, though the greater distance to European markets from Australia and New Zealand added enormously to the difficulties. Borthwicks in London were buying South American chilled beef regularly, and whenever anyone from Australia or New Zealand appeared at Audrey House Lord Whitburgh would ask why they didn't try their hand at this game.

Australia sent a trial shipment from the Moreton works in 1932 by the s.s. *Mooltan*. It was not a success: 70 per cent was condemned on arrival. But experiments continued. Portland sent six shipments in one year, and these were highly commended by the London dock authorities.

Meanwhile the New Zealand head office received a cable from London: 'Have arranged for the *Port Fairy* to have two lockers available for chilled beef.' Something had to be done then. Waingawa works handled the job. It was the first shipment of chilled beef from New Zealand for many years. And it was a tricky business. They used a spear thermometer to make sure that the carcases were kept within the necessary close limits of temperature; and, following the latest practice, carbon dioxide was introduced into the ship's lockers to check the growth of mould.

More shipments were made both from Australia and New Zealand. Other companies followed Borthwicks' lead, and by 1939, when chilling was stopped by Government because of the war, quite a sizeable trade in chilled beef had developed. New Zealand shipped 1,000 tons in the first year, 18,000 tons in the last year of peace. In the same time despatches from Australia increased from 3,000 to 27,000 tons. One reason why Borthwicks have been so much to the fore in this development lies in the fact that they have no permanent stake in South America.

Rabbits were a useful side-line both before, during and after the second world war. At one time the firm had rabbit works both in Australia and New Zealand—one near the southern border of Queensland, another in Otago, South Island. In Victoria buyers used to go round with vans equipped as portable chillers, collecting from local rabbit catchers and delivering the carcases to the meat works at Brooklyn and Portland. In New Zealand also two of the meat works used to handle rabbits. In total, New Zealand shipped an average of 42,000 cases in the 1930s, but this business has now ceased. Australia, on the other hand, has increased from a pre-war average of 220,000 cases to an average, at the time of writing, of 300,000 cases per annum.

Many of the works killed, as they do now, a certain number of pigs. Waitara had a bacon factory attached to it when Borthwicks took it over (it is in an important dairy farming district where pigs are kept to provide a profitable use for skim milk) and this still operates. New Zealand's slaughter of pigs has decreased from just under a million head to 860,000 and the export kill shows a dramatic drop from 650,000 in 1938 to about 70,000 head at the present time. Dairying interests have an assured income from the Statutory Board, and pigs, the dairyman's overtime, are no longer such a necessary side-line.

Far more important and more permanent as a factor in the business than all these are the by-products of the meat works. The number of hitherto wasted parts for which profitable uses were found increased continually, though science has expanded the list much more rapidly in recent years.

First in value is the first you come to when you start to deal with an animal in the slaughterhouse—the skin. Wool, hides and pelts (the stripped skins) have uses which are well known; as have casings (intestines), tallow, and the various inedible products that are made into fertiliser. Experts in the firm's offices will talk for hours on this subject, show you mountains of samples, describe their comparative qualities, the markets in which they may be sold, and the damage that can be done to the skins by grass seeds and to the hides by ticks while the animal is still at large. Every works has its fellmongery where the skins are treated to produce pelts and wool.

This last statement, however, must be qualified. In 1931 Borthwicks started sending dried sheepskins from the Australian works to Mazamet in France to be fellmongered by the brothers Martin-Estrabaud. Mazamet is one of those small towns that specialise. It has today some fifty fellmongeries which together deal with about twenty-five million skins a year, nearly half of which come from Australia. Its wool and 'slats' (dried pelts) are sold all over Europe.

The arrangement with Martin-Estrabaud continued and there will be more to say about it later.

Labour and the State

As to the men and their loyalty, enough has been said to show that Borthwicks have been as well served in Australia and New Zealand as in Britain. The response to emergency—the Hawke's Bay earthquake, fire at Waingawa—has always been magnificent. Though Monte Moss's record still stands, there is a longish list of men who hold the gold watch that is given in honour of long service. Everywhere there are families that have worked for the firm for three generations and are now represented by fathers and sons, uncles and nephews, brothers and cousins. Some of the older ones have memories, which have been handed on to their sons, nephews and grandchildren, of 'Lord Borthwick', Mr James, Mr William and Mr Algernon. The family tradition goes right through the ranks. It includes general managers—the Balderstones in Australia, the Normans in New Zealand.

The management came to good terms—it would have had to try to do so in any case—with the growing power of the Unions in both countries. Union representatives whom you meet around the works are generally reasonable men. They have the same feeling towards the firm as the rest; and some of them too are sons, nephews, brothers of other Borthwick men. They think of themselves as intermediaries. There are differences, of course: but these can usually be ironed out by amicable discussion.

Records of agreements with Unions go back a long way. In the Moreton works manager's office there is a copy of the very first 'Log of Wages'—a little printed booklet that records terms agreed at a conference towards the end of 1912 with the Australian Meat Employees' Union, to be operative throughout 1913. Normal hours, 48 per week: 7.30 to 5 p.m., 1 p.m. on Saturdays. One hour allowed for each meal and two 'smoke-o's' of 15 minutes each. Work on close holidays (such as Christmas Day and Good Friday) to be paid at double rates; on ordinary holidays (New Year, Easter Monday etc.) at 1½ times normal rates. Wages generally range from 8s. 7d. to 11s. 11d. for an eight-hour day.

Compare this with an award of 1931 (there are others in between, of course). The working week was by this time 44 hours; and wages in general were between 17s. and 25s. per day.

There was one big show-down. It came in the 1932–3 season and affected the whole meat industry both in Australia and New Zealand. First cause was the depression. The freezing works supported by Government (what else could they do?) cut down wage rates. The men, not unnaturally, did not appreciate the real position. They came out. In no time all the works were idle.

Borthwicks and other meat companies took the opportunity to instal the chain system, which they had been thinking of for some time. This did not add to the men's willingness to come back. They were suspicious of the new method—though here again they were playing King Canute: you can get in the way of change but you can't stop it. The strike went on for weeks.

Borthwicks called for volunteers to run the works. They got them: and so the chains were operated first by amateurs. To begin with they were anything but skilful and output was pathetically low. Also there were plenty of cut fingers: for butchers' knives are sharp. But they learned pretty quickly. The daily kill mounted steadily.

Brooklyn's story is typical of most works in both countries. Some 300 men worked, ate and slept on the premises. A kitchen was rigged up in the old garage and cooks were engaged. There was a small police garrison equipped with searchlights. (In the event no serious violence occurred.) The foremen carried bandages; there was sick parade every morning and the casualty station did good business in the beginning. The first day's kill was 33: the first week's, with one chain working, 4,500: in the fifth week, with three chains, they reached 45,000.

After this the regulars came back, except some older men who were too used to solo butchering to face the change. A sad story. But what would you? Change must come.

Experts say that the chain system has not increased output per man. But it has very substantially increased output in relation to space occupied: and this is equally vital in the economics of the business. It also demands fewer highly skilled men, involving more relatively unskilled jobs that a man can learn quickly.

The Governments of Australia and New Zealand have done a great deal to encourage the meat trade and there has been much fruitful co-operation. There have been, and are, some little difficulties, naturally. In Australia these have arisen mainly from the relations between the States, and between the States and the Commonwealth. Rail transport is not made easier by a change of gauge at State borders. Again, in the matter of wages and working conditions, there is sometimes a conflict between Government awards and State awards that are current at the same time, which can cause confusion.

Local regulations too, though no doubt there are reasons for them, may occasionally restrict activity. In Brisbane for instance (that is in the city itself) no meat may be sold to the public that has not been killed at the State Government's abattoir; and a similar franchise has been given abattoirs in other cities of Queensland to the detriment of private enterprise export works. This has particularly affected Borthwicks' Moreton works, which is less than a mile away from the Brisbane abattoir. The population of Brisbane has grown from 283,000 in 1930 to 635,000 in 1962 and many people obviously require a lot of meat. Strenuous efforts have been made by Borthwicks and other export companies to point out to the Government that the State of Queensland needs soundly based and economically operated export works to handle the flush of cattle which must go to export between March and September every year; and by not allowing these works to kill for the local trade, they are undermining their ability to handle the export beef economically. It was hoped that the recent Country Party/Liberal Party Government, which took office after twenty-five years of Labour rule in the State, would recognise this serious disadvantage to the private enterprise beef export industry, but the meat trade has been disappointed that this Government's attitude has been no different from that of previous Labour Governments. It stands to reason that a large capital city must have more than one abattoir supplying its meat; but while the present monopoly persists, the economics of the private export works are undermined.

New Zealand's trend towards what was called a socialistic outlook was referred to in an earlier chapter. This goes strangely with the people's sturdy independence. Yet both are legacies of history. After the pioneering days, when individualism was what won through, there came a time when men were driven to combine and called on the law to protect their rights. In such conditions enterprise sometimes attracts suspicion from official quarters. This perhaps was what was behind the holding back of the Waingawa licence. A more frustrating instance occurred a year before that. Borthwicks had bought two works—Ngahauranga and Kakariki—from the Wellington Meat Export Company and signed up to pay £200,000 for them. The Government refused to sanction the transfer. What rankled most was that another meat company was later allowed to lease Ngahauranga. Kakariki is now a woollen mill. This incident too helped to strengthen the directors' feeling that New Zealand was discriminating against 'overseas' companies.

Another instance of what at least looked like discrimination happened a few years later. During the early thirties the effects of the world slump were still being felt. In New Zealand all commodity prices were affected. There was despondency in the meat trade, and a feeling that there were too many freezing works for the numbers of livestock now coming on the market. This feeling was strongest in the South Island. There were seven works in the Canterbury district alone; and here it was even suggested that one or more works should be closed down.

Another proposal was that all the works in this district should accept a voluntary killing quota so that each of them would at least be assured of a fixed percentage of the total number of stock coming on the market.

Borthwicks have always believed (and their reasons are given in the last chapter) that private enterprise is best for the meat trade, and that if private enterprise is to work effectively it must be really competitive. They

START HERE   EXAMPLE OF A FREEZING WORK

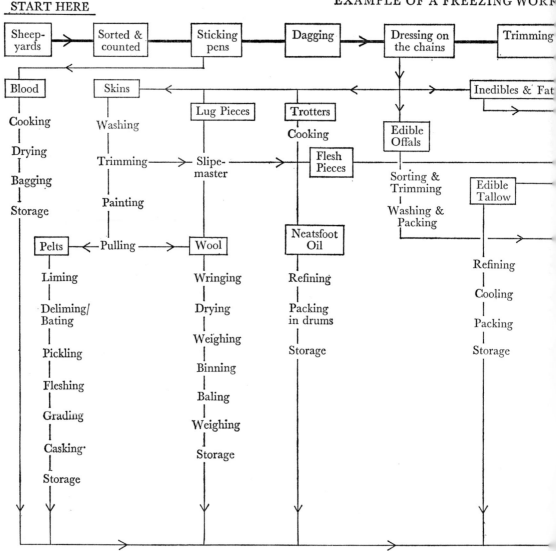

Note: The CARCASE MEAT flow is quite simply the top line reading from left to right. The chain system is described below. The vertical lines show how all the by-products and offal are treated and give a good impression of the complications involved.

The chain system of killing lamb or mutton (in England 'the line system') consists of a moving conveyor which carries the dead sheep, suspended by a hind leg, from the killing box through a trough (to collect the blood) into the main hall. In New Zealand, the process is as follows: a man opens up the skin on the hind legs; others open up the skin right

̖OW CHART FOR MUTTON AND LAMB

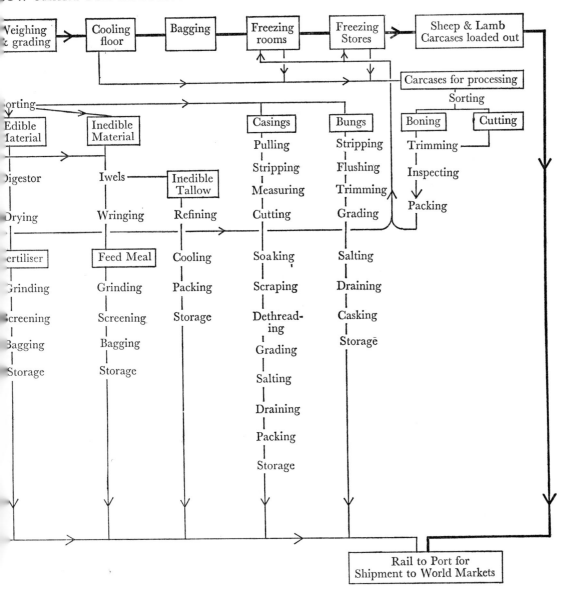

̖Veighing & grading	Cooling floor	Bagging	Freezing rooms	Freezing Stores	Sheep & Lamb Carcases loaded out

Carcases for processing

Sorting

̖orting

̖Edible ̖Material	Inedible Material		Casings	Bungs	Boning	Cutting
			Pulling	Stripping	Trimming	
			Stripping	Flushing	Inspecting	
̖Digestor	Iwels	Inedible Tallow	Measuring	Trimming	Packing	
̖Drying	Wringing	Refining	Cutting	Grading		
̖ertiliser	Feed Meal	Cooling	Soaking	Salting		
̖Grinding	Grinding	Packing	Scraping	Draining		
̖creening	Screening	Storage	Dethreading	Casking		
̖Bagging	Bagging		Grading	Storage		
̖Storage	Storage		Salting			
			Draining			
			Packing			
			Storage			

Rail to Port for
Shipment to World Markets

down the stomach, brisket and front legs; the shoulders are then cleared and the tongue and head removed; the brisket is chopped through; the skin is pulled off; the carcase is opened up and the pluck removed; the carcase is now pressure-washed, wiped down and dried off; skirt removed and ticket hole made, rough edges trimmed; the neck is tied to front legs, and wiped to remove any excess blood. The carcase is then weighed and graded. Each motion is carried out by one or more men as the carcase moves slowly along the conveyor chain from the slaughter floor away to the cooling room, being sorted according to grade and brand before being put in a stockinette wrapper and run into the freezing rooms.

refused to have anything to do with any such 'stay-put' arrangement and continued to pay what they thought reasonable for livestock.

It happened that at this very time most works in New Zealand—as indeed in Australia also—were in the middle of the change-over to the chain system of slaughtering. Under the old solo system each company had been licensed to carry a specified number of hooks; and this enabled the Meat Board to regulate, more or less, the number of stock each company could kill. When the chain system came along some people thought (erroneously) that there would no longer be any limit on the number of stock a works could kill, and that if one company were to take advantage of this in a time of shortage one or other works might not get enough stock to be able to carry on. Someone (gifted with a strong imagination) actually raised the bogy that Borthwicks might squeeze out the New Zealand-owned companies and so get complete control of the South Island business!

In 1934 the 'quota' companies (as we may conveniently call them) took the extreme step of appealing to the New Zealand Government, who, on the recommendation of the Meat Producers' Board, passed the Slaughtering and Amendment Act. Soon afterwards a killing quota was imposed on Borthwicks' Belfast works—but not on any of the other works in the Canterbury district. It is significant that Borthwicks were the only British company operating in the South Island: had the row been between different New Zealand companies the Government might not have intervened. At any rate, there is no record to show that they ever put a quota on any New Zealand-owned company.

This singling out of Borthwicks was strongly criticised by many farmers at the time. And indeed the main result was, beyond doubt, that for several years the Canterbury farmers were paid rather less for their stock than they would have been if Borthwicks had been free to operate competitively as they had always done.

In time the 'restriction mentality' went out of fashion; though Borthwicks' quota was not removed until some years after the second world war. The unhappy incident is now long past. Relations between the meat companies are now fully competitive, and the situation in the Canterbury district today is altogether healthier.

Thirty years later a historian may perhaps be permitted some thoughts on this rather extraordinary affair. It must be remembered that Borthwicks was run by three middle-aged men who had spent their formative years before 1914. Free trade, freely convertible currency, a gold standard, free competition and the power of the market were in their minds, the Ark of the Covenant. They strongly disapproved of the restrictive mentality of the inter-war years and considered that it was the cause of the stagnation and slow development that was the feature of those days. (It is of course very questionable whether their own remedies would have worked if they had been tried.)

It was always certain that, with this background and this business philosophy, they would disapprove, on what they regarded as ethical grounds, of the get-together that was here suggested. However, the real criticism that may be made of them is not that they were wrong, but that they were unaware of what was actually happening. The world was changing and they were unaware of the change; and restrictive practices that no one would have dreamt of any Government tolerating, let alone actively supporting, before 1914 were looked upon with favour in the inter-war years. New Zealand was not alone in this. A dramatic instance in the United Kingdom was the closure of the Jarrow shipbuilding yards epitomized in *The Death of a Town*; but the three middle-aged men running Borthwicks lived in a sort of ivory tower and were quite unaware of this current of opinion.

The 'quota' companies, as a matter of normal commercial relationship, should surely have approached Borthwicks before appealing to the Government for protection from the hazard of normal competition. That they did not do so may have been due to the move of the Head Office from Christchurch to Masterton which gave a further impression of ivory tower aloofness. While what follows is guesswork, it seems probable that the New Zealand Government and/or the Meat Board hoped that Borthwicks would join the quota but did not like to say so as it would be tantamount to encouraging lower prices to the producers. It is at any rate an explanation of what seemed to Borthwicks at the time a very strange performance, namely a Government encouraging operators to combine in order to pay producers a lower price than normal competition would have secured.

The faint aura of suspicion towards private enterprise and towards 'overseas' companies persists in New Zealand. Borthwicks have not suffered from any further evidences of discrimination, but occasional speeches by public men continue to emphasise that suspicion towards successful enterprise and towards 'overseas' companies still exists.

Fortunately the firm's relations with 'outside' works remain as good as ever. Thus even in those parts of New Zealand—they are very large and

Sundowner

very productive—that are not within reach of any Borthwick works the buying organisation is kept busy. Besides this the firm has arrangements with certain 'outside' companies, which do their own livestock buying, to take over the whole or part of their output.

In describing the formation of T. B. & S. (Australasia) back in 1905 some remarks were made about taxation and its influence on decisions. Changed conditions have complicated things considerably. At that time the firm's business consisted mainly of selling Australian and New Zealand meat in Britain on commission, though it had already acquired its first freezing works. Gradually it became a substantial organisation buying livestock from farmers, killing them in its own chain of works which employed large numbers of men, and dealing with 'outside' works also. A very much larger proportion of its profits were attributable to Australia and New Zealand. At an early stage the tax authorities in these countries quite naturally thought that they were entitled to a larger share; and as time went on they paid more and more attention to the firm's activities. Some of the questions they asked were difficult to answer and some impossible.

For example, one specially persistent State tax man in Australia wanted to know at what price the meat was eventually sold. It is always difficult to put a value on imported meat, which is rarely sold the day after it arrives. Frozen beef in particular may be kept in cold store for as much as six months. Borthwicks had branches and depots all over Britain and much of the meat was cut up and the cuts sold at different times. So the question was difficult to answer. In fact the firm's auditors certified that it was impossible. Even so, it took some years to convince the tax man.

The many problems that arose very largely disappeared with the introduction of Double Taxation Relief in 1946 and the completion of tax conventions between the United Kingdom and Australia and New Zealand. Borthwicks now do what they probably should have done from the start: they take over all meat at the official price quoted by the Imported Meat Trade Association at the time of its arrival. If T. B. & S. (Australasia) can make money on that, the profit—and, if not, the loss—is theirs. This arrangement appears to satisfy the tax authorities in all three countries.

Some Statistical Notes

Bowen Works, Queensland, was bought from Bergls in 1933 for £A.21,000. Its book value now is nearly £A.500,000. The kill has fluctuated considerably over the last thirty years, but recently it has been about 45,000 cattle a year.

Waingawa Works, near Masterton in the North Island of New Zealand, was bought in 1928 from the Wairarapa Farmers' Meat Company for £120,000. Much has also been done to this works, which is valued in the books today at over £900,000. It now kills about 500,000 sheep and lamb and 40,000 cattle a year.

Feilding Works, in the Manawatu district of the North Island of New Zealand, was bought from the Feilding Farmers' Freezing Company in 1931 for £100,000. Now valued in the books at over £900,000, its annual kill is some 750,000 sheep and lamb and 35,000 cattle.

CHAPTER NINE

Second World War

On the evening of Friday, the 1st September 1939, when the thousands of workers at Smithfield were looking forward to their well earned two-day week-end, they heard the radio asking them all to report for duty next morning, Saturday. When they came in next morning every piece of equipment in every stall—scales, chopping blocks, meat hooks and so on—had a tag on it with the name of some place on the perimeter of London such as Earl's Court, Lewisham or Islington. Soon vans were going round the market, the drivers stopping at each stall and calling out: 'Anything for Earl's Court?' or: 'Anything for Lewisham?'—each van collecting the things labelled for one place.

On Sunday, the 3rd September, the Prime Minister announced that Britain and Germany were at war.

The next day, Monday, Smithfield was empty and silent. It remained so, except that the poultry market was opened for dealings in such unrationed items as poultry and rabbits, throughout the war. But the citizens of London and the people of Britain were never without meat. Those who lived alone found that their rations did not go far; but millions probably fed better, and many certainly had a better balanced diet, than they had in peace time. This was due partly to rationing, partly to the organisation that the country's meat industry worked out and had ready against the emergency.

The two most important parts of this organisation, so far as imported meat was concerned, were known by the mystic names MINDAL and LWMSA—the initials of the Meat Importers' National Defence Association Limited and the London Wholesale Meat Supply Association respectively. Planning started during the Munich period, at least eighteen months before war broke out. MINDAL's function has been described as 'warehouseman for the Ministry of Food'. It made allocations of imported meat (it had nothing to do with home killed) to LWMSA and the other regional bodies that were formed as soon as LWMSA had learned and coped with most of the main snags. The regional Meat Supply Associations, which were subdivided into butchers' committees representing groups of shops, handled both imported and home killed meat. Allocation to butchers in proportion to their previous consumption started as soon as war was declared. Rationing of consumers was introduced a month or two later.

The closing of Smithfield for meat dealing and the decentralisation to some thirty improvised depots in cold stores or adapted garages round the edge of London (such places as Earl's Court and Islington) was organised by LWMSA in the anticipation that as soon as war broke out the capital would be well and truly bombed—which in fact did not happen until later. On that Saturday morning, the 2nd September, every person at Smithfield over thirty, except a few picked key men, was given a slip saying that as from Monday morning he would be employed and paid by LWMSA and would work at a stated depot—usually the one nearest to his own home. Depot staffs were carefully chosen so that, for instance, the manager and cashier at any depot were never employees of the same firm.

MINDAL took over the whole meat cargoes of ships that were at the wharf in London and other ports. Some of these carried big quantities of chilled beef, which their captains were ordered by radio to freeze down. That was the end of chilling for the duration, and in fact until meat was decontrolled.

Borthwicks and the war in London

Soon there was little left of Borthwicks in London. R. G. Bremner was chief executive officer to LWMSA through its crucial teething period. Then he was given the same appointment with MINDAL. Joe Curley, who before this was assistant market manager under Bremner and had been drawn into the defence planning organisation, was drafted on the outbreak of war to Mill Hill as distribution officer to LWMSA. In 1942 he was called up: but

Bremner, who was then with MINDAL in North Wales, got the Ministry of Food to have his call-up cancelled, and he was then asked to manage MINDAL's London office in St. Martin's-le-Grand. William Miles, who had been seconded to help the Ministry, became office manager to LWMSA.

Others of the staff too served in these organisations. Many more of course went into the Services, including the younger generation of Borthwicks—Algy, Jason, Peter and John. What work was left for the firm itself to do—and this included sharing with a rival firm, Weddels, the heavy task of meat distribution to the Forces in Britain—was still directed by Lord Whitburgh and his brothers James and Algernon. Algernon, however, died after a long illness in 1942.

The universal slogan was 'Out of London'. As soon as war was declared about 1,000 tons of meat had been evacuated over the week-end from Borthwick Wharf to outlying cold stores at such places as Southampton. When the bombing really started most of what remained of head office followed the Ministry of Food and MINDAL's headquarters to the comparative peace and security of North Wales; they settled in Colwyn Bay under the secretary, Savage.

A few, however, stuck it out at Audrey House. Among them was Eric Watson, who had been in charge of accounts at Smithfield, and was retained as a key man at the Ministry's request. One of his war-time jobs was to see that accounts due to the firm from butchers were paid. This was quite an undertaking; for as soon as LWMSA started up all meat had to be paid for in cash, which generally meant that the first week's deliveries were paid for with the money that should have gone to pay for the previous week's purchases on Smithfield, where dealings were on weekly credit terms. He says it was astonishing what efforts butchers made to clear these outstanding accounts in spite of war-time difficulties such as bad debts due to evacuation. Almost all of them did so in the end, though in some cases it took a couple of years. Meanwhile Watson kept the books.

Another of his jobs was the allocation of poultry and rabbits, which it was decided about that time to distribute through Smithfield. The rabbits came from Australia until the U-boats got going, after which they were shipped from Ireland. They were doled out to shops in proportion to their pre-war purchases. There was a big demand for them from people who had despised them in easier times: but Watson was careful to see that old rabbit customers, including London's barrow boys, got their fair share.

He and the small staff that remained with him were receiving a number of visitors, among whom they remember particularly the New Zealand Air Force men on short leave. They all knew about Borthwicks and, when at a loose end in a strange land, gravitated to Audrey House—a link with home.

Watson has an old book which consists of carbon copies of the letters he wrote to Savage at Colwyn Bay between September 1940 and February 1941—a time when typists were hard to get, and also when the bombing of London was at its peak. They were written by hand, many of them in air-raid shelters. Here are extracts:

12/9/40. The block opposite Ely Place have lost most of their glass. This was the nearest I know to Audrey House. . . . I passed two D/As (delayed action bombs) cordoned off in my 300-yard walk to Bayswater station this morning, and on arrival there found the booking-office had received one to itself and no trains were running. . . . Last night's barrage was simply terrific from 9 p.m. until about 5 a.m.

18/9/40. As you know, the whole corner of the Market was taken off last Wednesday. On Monday night they had thirty to forty incendiaries on the Market roof. The fire brigade got them in hand at once. . . . Of course, the Market was flooded with water.

26/9/40. I had intended to spend some time with Chappell at 264 . . . but it was quite impossible. I finally got him to bring his papers over to Audrey House and spent an hour or two in the A.R. Shelter during a warning writing out the Ledger, etc.

30/12/40. This morning Mr. Welch arrived at 10.45 (having left Kingston 7 a.m.) and Mr Cooper at 11.15 (having left Croydon at 8 a.m.). Last night's raid on the City was one of the severest yet. From outside it appeared as though the whole City were ablaze. An H.E. bomb . . . has blown out most of the windows in Ely Place. . . . Audrey House miraculously escaped damage.

Such was life in London during the winter of 1940. After Germany attacked Russia there was a lull for a couple of years. Work went on. It was mostly connected with the continually increasing sale of rabbits, liaison with MINDAL and LWMSA, and keeping in touch with Colwyn Bay. 'Mr. James', who lived at Fox Hills, near Reading, was often at Audrey House. Most of the firm's records had been sent to Fox Hills for safety.

Then the bombing started again. Watson's later letters refer to the 'scalded cat' raids of early 1943 and to further narrow escapes for Audrey House. Then, in February 1944:

These last few raids seem to have affected people more than the 1940/41 blitz. I suppose this is due to the long lull, general war-weariness and—above all—to the size of the stuff that is being used. The blast-area of the H.E. is much bigger and the incendiaries are being dropped in canisters containing 30, 70 or even more. . . . Mr James was in this morning and told me that all his farm buildings had been demolished by one bomb, and all his windows blown in as the result of another, but no casualties, even to the stock. Our safe-keeping records were not so safe as we had imagined.

(The second of these bombs in fact hit an ammunition dump which blew up. It was one of the biggest bangs of the war.)

In June of that year comes the first reference to pilotless aircraft—the 'doodle-bugs'. Audrey House has suffered damage but this is limited to two windows. Borthwick Wharf is all right. (It had had twenty-five doodle-bugs within 600 yards but not one touched it.)

In September 1944 there is a report of mysterious explosions, far louder than any flying bomb, preceded by no sirens and no warning sound at all. Official silence on the subject was causing all sorts of rumours. . . . The mystery was explained at length. These were the V2s. They were Germany's last kick at England.

Audrey House suffered some more damage before the end but nothing serious. A 1,000-lb. bomb dropped alongside Borthwick Wharf and caused some trouble, but the reinforced concrete stood up to it remarkably well.

In Liverpool

At the Liverpool branch a skeleton staff carried on under the manager, J. L. Sharman. The Ministry took over cold storage, and private sales were virtually confined, as in London, to poultry and rabbits. There was a great deal of work in maintaining supplies to the Forces, including in the later stages the Americans, and to the enormous number of aliens interned in the Isle of Man. It is the branch's pride that no soldier, sailor, airman or civilian ever went without a meal through their failure. They always supplied the required amount; though sometimes it had to be mutton instead of beef.

After about a year of bombing the Port of London was so knocked about that most imported meat was being landed at Liverpool, though some went to Glasgow and Avonmouth. In any case Liverpool was an important industrial town and port: and it was not surprising that the *Luftwaffe* should pay it the compliment of their attentions.

It soon became known among German bomber pilots that Liverpool was 'a piece of cake'. In the early stages it had no anti-aircraft defence at all except barrage balloons. The first raid, which J. L. Sharman remembers well, was made in broad daylight and the 'planes were quite unmolested. At night they used to come across the Irish Sea, taking their bearings on Dublin, which was not blacked out. Later, Liverpool got plenty of Ack-Ack guns and, later still, rocket-firing Z batteries.

The worst was over before then. Seven nights of intensive bombing in May 1941 left the docks and the city a mass of flames which there was no water to fight. The enemy came low enough to machine-gun people in the streets. Several Borthwick vans were hit. If the bombing had gone on one more week Liverpool would have been finished. But for no apparent reason it stopped.

The Lancashire Cold Store must, as Sharman puts it, 'have been hung with horseshoes'. It was untouched, though there was devastation and death all around, and the firm's office and garage which had been attached to it were in ruins. There were no casualties among the staff.

A big S O S came through just after D-day. Some forty or fifty American refrigerated vans, each with a capacity of about five tons, had to be loaded at once with meat for the troops in France. The skeleton staff, who had been working all day, responded nobly and worked through the night. They got all the vans loaded and away to France by morning.

So Borthwicks in Liverpool, as in London, had good reason to be thankful for having come through the bombing with comparatively little damage, and good reason to be proud of the job that those who saw the war through there did in extremely severe conditions.

One rather unexpected result of the war so far as Borthwicks were concerned was that money accumulated. In peace time, of course, livestock was paid for when it was bought from the farmers. The money was not recovered until the meat was sold to butchers in Britain: and considerable resources were needed to finance the long time-lag between paying out the money and getting it back. But while controls were in force, the bulk-purchasing authorities in Australia and New Zealand paid for all meat at a stated interval after it was bought. So a large part of these resources was not required. Some of the money was invested in gilt edged. Some of it—half a million pounds—was lent without interest to the Government as an extra contribution from Borthwicks towards the war.

Another fund which had to be kept in reserve consisted of the very considerable sums normally spent every year on maintenance of the works and plant. All this work was inevitably suspended for the duration; meanwhile the works were at least as hard pressed as in peace time. It would obviously have to be done one day—and, in fact, it had to be done at greatly increased prices. This gave rise to difficulties which will be referred to later.

In Australia and New Zealand

In Australia and New Zealand plans made in advance came into force when the war began. Bulk purchase was applied not only to meat but also to wool and pelts. Prices were fixed and there was no competition. Nevertheless the meat companies had plenty of problems to cope with. Manpower troubles were only to be expected. Many trained workers joined the Forces. They were replaced partly by bringing in men from the farms—who were soon directed back to help keep up the livestock supply. In the end the works were employing virtually anyone they could get.

One of the worst difficulties was shortage of ships, particularly after the U-boats got going. In case of serious shipping hold-ups it was ordered that every works should have enough storage space for 60 per cent of a whole season's kill. As many of the larger works could, and often did, kill 6,000 in a day, this called for considerable extensions. It happened that New Zealand as a whole had about a million carcases in store when the war started—a fortunate chance; but these had to be shipped as quickly as possible to make room for more.

An experimental war measure was the dehydration of mutton, for the Forces in particular. The Dominion Governments built dehydrating plants at three Borthwick works—Portland and Moreton in Australia and Feilding in New Zealand; and these the firm operated. The dehydrated meat, of the consistency of currants, was packed in 25-lb. tins. A good deal of it went to the troops in New Guinea. It was not a great success: its taste has been described as 'like eating sawdust'. Borthwicks took over the plants after the war and adapted them for other purposes.

An expedient to save freezing space was the 'telescoping' of lambs—cutting off the hindquarters and putting them inside the trunks. This was started early on in Australia by order of the Commonwealth Government: Brooklyn shipped its first telescoped lambs on the *Themistocles* in December 1939.

The firm's offices in both countries, with depleted staffs, had more than enough to do looking after the introduction of special measures, keeping the works going in spite of manpower troubles, and maintaining the flow of livestock; though buying was simplified by fixed price schedules and by the arrangement that each company kept its pre-war clients. Buyers were allowed to join up; and if they did so the firm kept their jobs open for them, paying half their salaries to their wives or dependants meanwhile.

Pat Borthwick remained as family resident director, his efforts to join the New Zealand Forces overseas having been stymied by the authorities, who considered him indispensable where he was. He had the invaluable support of James Balderstone in Australia. Ted Norman was taken from New Zealand in 1941 and stayed away for the duration: but a most able deputy for him was found in Arthur Corskie, who saw the job through, and was afterwards stock manager in the New Zealand head office until 1962, when he became livestock consultant to the firm.

Norman was lent to the British Ministry of Food and went to Buenos Aires as their representative in South America. (Two letters from war-time Ministers of Food—Lord Woolton and Lord Llewellin—thanking him for the three-and-a-half-years' work he did there are now in the Waingawa works office.)

Besides the continual effort to get as much frozen beef, mutton and lamb as possible away to Britain, and deliveries under contract to the British, Australian and United States Navies at any hour of the day or night, the Australian works were active in the export of rabbits. Portland started shipping butter also in 1939. This was resumed after the war and shipments averaged 3,000 tons a year.

During these years the firm in Australia was developing its local trade, mainly with wholesalers, though it also opened a retail shop in Brisbane. This last was primarily for the convenience of ships in war-time, though it carried on until 1949 serving the public.

The chief war-time development by the firm in New Zealand was a big extension at Waitara, which incidentally involved an unusual piece of engineering and a special Act of Parliament. The slaughterhouse was moved to the other side of Queen Street, which runs past the works. The dressing of carcases remained on the original side, with the result that now thousands of freshly killed beasts are conveyed every day across a public highway—in fact over the top of it by a modern version of the Bridge of Sighs so well known to tourists in Venice. It was this that called for special legislation, which was passed without difficulty. The enclosed overhead ramp through which the carcases travel by mechanical conveyor, being cleansed as they go by sprays of water, was constructed in 1940. Its concrete floor was poured in one day and is fitted with an expansion joint, thus preventing the possibility of a drip on the innocent heads of Waitara's townspeople.

Within a year after the ramp came into use Percy Allen, who had been works manager at Waitara for more than twenty years by that time, woke up at four o'clock one morning to hear a loud crackling noise in the distance. He thought the Japanese had landed: but it was another fire at the works. The noise was made by the asbestos roof cracking under the heat. The outbreak was in the wool section of the fellmongery. It was not serious enough to stop killing; but for some time wool was spread out in the town's public streets and recreation ground.

In 1944, before the end of the war, Borthwicks bought yet another works in the North Island—Tokomaru Bay, on the coast about thirty-five miles south of East Cape and a good deal farther north than any of their existing works. This was the only one that did not justify itself. Most of the land in its buying area had been leased from the Maoris. New Zealand's Labour Government decreed that when the leases ran out possession should be restored to the owners. Many of them were not so keen on intensive live-stock production. Tokomaru Bay's intake dwindled year by year until eventually it was closed down.

Australia and New Zealand, apart from the distinguished fighting record of their armies, navies and air forces, including Maori units, had served the Allies well by supplying essential food in spite of the U-boats and other enemy attacks at sea. During these years Britain received 837,000 tons of meat from Australia and 1,654,000 tons from New Zealand. This does not include large supplies to Allied Service units in various parts of the world.

In all this the firm had played its part. Its able-bodied men and women, except those who were retained as indispensable to an essential industry, had served in the Forces; and those who remained had stood the strains— often no less cruel than battle—of bombing, fire watching and A.R.P. Many had lost their lives. Two members of the Borthwick family were killed during the invasion of Europe. One was James's younger son Peter. The other was Walter Hazell, son of Letitia (fourth child of Thomas and Letitia Borthwick) and Ernest Hazell.

The name of Hazell, incidentally, is also connected with a family business, though this, unlike Borthwicks, is now a public company. The firm of Hazell Watson & Viney designed and printed this book.

CHAPTER TEN

Nine More Years Under Controls

The end of the war in 1945 did not mean a return to peace-time conditions for the meat trade. Rationing remained in force and MINDAL and LWMSA continued to function. The garages around London that had been converted into meat depots were now wanted by their owners, so LWMSA moved to Smithfield, using two of the markets as its distribution centre. The other two were used for dealing in unrationed goods; and there Borthwicks had one stall, where they sold such products of Australia and New Zealand as poultry and rabbits. So things went on until decontrol in 1954.

It was a rather strange world, so far as business was concerned, that greeted returning warriors as they came back to Audrey House one by one. No doubt they, and the handful who had seen the war through in London, looked at one another, each thinking: 'He seems older than I remember him.' And no doubt they all thought of those who would never come back.

Algy Borthwick, a Territorial before the war, had spent most of the last six years with the London Scottish as an infantry company commander. He had been wounded in Italy and was awarded an M.C. Jason had served in anti-submarine trawlers and aircraft carriers with the R.N.V.R. and won a D.S.C. John had been with the Rifle Brigade (as his uncle William had during the first world war), rising from rifleman to major. He was soon off to the United States, Australia and New Zealand.

Alec Fyffe's four years in Japanese hands had left him in poor health. After a year spent partly with MINDAL and partly in hospital, he returned to his pre-war interests of market statistics and costing. Things being as they were, his activities for a time were mainly concerned with rabbits. Later on he too paid a visit to Australia and New Zealand.

Some of those who were with the control organisations did not come back for some time. William Miles, for instance, was retained by LWMSA until decontrol. On the other hand the Ministry released Joe Curley in September 1945. The firm then sent him to Australia and New Zealand. But when he came home in 1947, MINDAL being very short-staffed, the Ministry borrowed him back again for a couple of years. Algy Borthwick became chairman of MINDAL until it was disbanded.

Meanwhile enquiries were coming in from valued pre-war customers, while other old friends had either disappeared or for various reasons were not yet in the market. New outlets had to be found against the time when controls should be removed, and a new sales organisation built up; all this with many experienced members of the team either otherwise engaged for the time or gone for good. What trade could be done during this period of semi-suspension was hampered by controls and exchange regulations, not only in Britain but in all countries.

The second generation of Borthwicks was now getting on in years and, with the third generation back from the war, the time had come for another gradual handing over of control. Lord Whitburgh's heart—that part of it that was not in the business—was, like his father's, in farming and the Midlothian estate. He spent more and more of his time at Whitburgh. Very soon he retired there altogether, vacating the chairmanship of Borthwicks and T. B. & S. (Australasia) in favour of his nephew Algy, the eldest of the third generation. James never really recovered from the shock of his younger son's death. He himself died peacefully in 1961. William, it will be remembered, had taken no active part in the business since before the first world war, and Algernon had died in 1942.

Lord Whitburgh continued to take much more than a theoretical interest in quality beef production. He pioneered his own ideas on the subject. Though at the time of this book's publication he is in his ninetieth year, the work goes on—and still very definitely under his personal control. Whitburgh not only breeds cattle in the Scottish tradition, based on the blue-grey cow and the Aberdeen Angus bull, but fattens them, sends them to Edinburgh for slaughter and then to Smithfield—in essence the same integrated operation as starts on Borthwicks' Australian cattle stations. It is believed that Whitburgh turns off more fat cattle than any other single farm in Britain.

The change in control at the top went as far as the secretary. S. E. H. Savage retired in 1952, having served the firm faithfully and ably for thirty-three years and headed the office at Colwyn Bay through the second world war. He kept his interest in Borthwicks; indeed he was then appointed financial adviser to the firm, and for some years afterwards would come at intervals to lunch with the directors at Audrey House. So, if it is correct that he first worked on the audit as an articled clerk in 1900, his association with the firm must have covered altogether about sixty years. His place as secretary was taken by W. S. McCrae.

So long as controls were on, finance continued on the same basis and money still accumulated. To this was added the half-million pounds lent interest-free to the Government and now repaid. When hostilities ended, there were certain jobs that had to be tackled immediately, particularly in making good the deferred maintenance of buildings and plant in Australia and New Zealand resulting from six years of flat-out working without normal maintenance and replacement. Some money went into improvements to the works such as extension of storage space to cope with increased killings: and part into new developments.

Incidentally the accumulated funds did not go anything like as far as might have been expected. All the deferred maintenance had to be carried out at prices that were several times above pre-war level; and of course the same applied to improvements. This is not the place to expatiate on the problem of maintaining and replacing fixed assets in a time of inflation (the effect of which is that money you save up to pay for such essential work is always worth a lot less when you come to spend it than it was when you put it in the bank). On the other hand it is a very important problem: it is a problem which almost all firms have had to face in these post-war years: it is frequently misunderstood; and Governments and tax inspectors sometimes seem to forget the great difficulties it involves. For these reasons Borthwicks' experiences in coping with it are dealt with, for the benefit of anyone interested, at some length in the last chapter—where will be found disquisitions on several subjects which are essential parts of the background but do not strictly belong to the story.

Restoration work in Britain was largely covered by war damage claims. These were comparatively small. Borthwick Wharf had not suffered much from the 1,000-lb. bomb that dropped near it. The Liverpool office and garage were replaced. In addition a canteen was built high on the roof of the Lancashire Cold Store for the staff, with a room for table tennis and other recreations during the lunch break. So the Liverpool branch, at any rate, was better off than before.

The repayment of another debt came as a pleasant surprise. In 1939 Martin-Estrabaud were still fellmongering Australian skins at Mazamet. When France fell they owed Borthwicks rather more than six million francs, which the firm naturally wrote off. After the war a letter from Martin-Estrabaud announced that they had managed to conceal the existence of this money from the Germans by investing it in real estate; as a result of which Borthwicks were now the owners of an hotel in Marseilles and a toy-shop.

This property was promptly sold—unfortunately for 'blocked' francs: but this does not lessen the credit due to the French firm for their scrupulous honesty and cleverness.

The arrangements at Mazamet were changed in 1948, when Borthwicks started a subsidiary there called T. B. & S. (France). This company, though it handles a substantial amount of business, is not large in numbers; consisting of a manager, E. H. Gavan, and a small office—which, incidentally, is run by Madame Gavan. It buys Australian skins (it can only do so if it offers the works a better price than they can get in Australia) and either re-sells them, or has them fellmongered on commission by local firms in the town and sells the wool and slats. It is a job that depends very largely on accurate judgment of prices, generally a longish time in advance.

The negotiations leading up to this new departure were conducted by John Borthwick, who has the advantage of fluent French. He spent a good deal of his time in France during the six years following his return from Australia and New Zealand.

In Australia

Immediately after the war James Balderstone retired. The loss was felt equally by all who had worked under him and by the directors. But he had certainly earned his leisure. Few can claim to have carried such responsibilities, and carried them so ably, through two world wars and the years between.

G. B. Robertson, who had been an outstanding works superintendent for the past eighteen years, succeeded him and carried on through most of the period covered by this chapter, which brought some big changes and developments. He retired owing to ill health in 1953 and died in 1961.

Robertson's successor was another James Balderstone, always known as Jim to solve the familiar problem of distinguishing fathers from sons. Jim Balderstone had joined Borthwicks before the second world war and, after serving in the Royal Australian Navy, spent the intervening years getting to know the job. He is a man born (as how could he help being?) with the business in his blood; and this includes land and livestock. Like Thomas Borthwick and three generations of his descendants, he is a farmer in what spare time he has.

S. F. Olliff, who started as a Smithfield salesman and came to Australia before the war as assistant general manager under James Balderstone, had been killed in action in Malaya. He was not replaced for the time being. His name, however, is remembered.

A new appointment was created in the Melbourne office in 1953—that of administrative manager. It was filled, and is still held, by P. F. J. Kendall. Before this he was with Deloitte, Plender, Griffiths & Company and had worked on the Borthwick audit for many years; though he was in Canada when Borthwicks invited him to go to Australia.

Continued controls on meat exports did not lessen the works' appetite for livestock nor the demands on the buying organisation; and one of the first reforms seen through by Robertson in Australia, as by Ted Norman in New Zealand, was the appointment of district managers as a link between the offices and groups of buyers. This step was called for by increasing purchases and increasing livestock production. Today the district manager is almost as well known to the farmers—the 'clients'—in his district as the buyers themselves. He has the advantage of getting to know at first hand the farmers' needs, problems and ideas over a wider area than any individual buyer; and he is in the best position to keep the farmers informed —whether directly or through the buyers—of the meat industry's aims and difficulties and the state of the market.

A lot of money was being spent in the post-war years, as we have said, on bringing all the freezing works up to their pre-war condition and better. To these outgoings were added the effects of another fire which broke out at the Moreton works, Brisbane, in 1946 and completely destroyed a cold store. It was an old wooden building and would have needed a great deal spent on it in any case; but the following figures further illustrate the problem of replacing worn-out assets in conditions of inflation. The store had been written down in the books to £11,000; it was insured for £80,000; and the new store, in concrete, cost £300,000.

One of the biggest headaches during these immediate post-war years in Australia and New Zealand was the state of mind of labour in general. The growing power of the unions has been referred to and it has been said that they did much good work. The chief trouble now was that they seemed to lose control of their own members.

It must be admitted that the men deserved a good deal of sympathy, for there were numbers of disturbing factors operating. Money was worth less and less. The price of wool, which is the basis of Australia's economy, rose to seven or eight times its pre-war level. And Communist agitators were active. The people of Australia about this time have been described as 'over-paid, over-taxed and bewildered'. The main result of all this, for the meat industry as for others, was an outbreak of 'go-slows' and strikes which did nothing but harm.

One of these strikes started in 1946 in a bacon factory in Queensland over the dismissal of some employees for pilfering; it spread to the other bacon factories and then to the meat works. It led to the union being de-registered and a new union formed. While it lasted Moreton carried on with a volunteer crew made up by members of the works staff, killed more than 9,000 sheep and lambs, and played a large part in keeping the citizens of Brisbane supplied with meat.

The firm in Australia had a big year of expansion in 1948: two more works and two more big cattle stations. So far the stock bought in Western Australia had all been killed in 'outside' works at Albany and Fremantle, an office in Perth looking after the buyers and handling shipments. Now Borthwicks bought Albany, a small works near the extreme south-western tip of the continent, from the Government of Western Australia.

Albany works had had a varied career since it was built by the State about 1910 for the use of fruit growers. It became a butter and cheese factory for a time. In 1935 it was leased to a company formed by local people to freeze fat lambs for export. During the war it was taken over by the State and extended to deal with cattle and pigs also. Its potential at the time it was offered for sale was promising. There was a big scheme to settle ex-Service men on farms in the south-west, and roads were being improved. Other considerations too appealed to Borthwicks. From Bowen to Albany they would have works spaced at intervals along nearly 3,000 miles of Australia's coastline. This would be convenient for ships, which usually, unless they are fully laden, work round from port to port, picking up cargoes as they go. Further, Albany's killing season being different from the other works, supplies would be available over a longer period of the year.

The promise has already begun to materialise. Before 1948 Albany's peak kill, achieved in one year during the war, was just over 56,000 lambs. Since then its annual total, including sheep, lambs, pigs and beef, has exceeded 200,000. Its stock is mostly drawn from within a radius of 50 miles—a big contrast with Queensland. The sheep are mostly merinos, big framed for the breed, which are being crossed with English rams to produce good fat lambs. This works also serves the fruit industry, as it did originally. In the last fourteen years it has stored an average of 30,000 cases of apples a year, with a peak of 57,000 in 1961–62. Most of these were subsequently shipped to Britain.

The second works that the firm bought in the same year was Yahl, near Mount Gambier, in the extreme south-east of South Australia, and not far from Portland. This was different from the other Borthwick works, being concerned at the time with bacon and smallgoods (sausages and other pre-pared meats) for the local trade. It had been started in 1900 by the Yahl Co-operative Cheese and Butter Company. Bacon was added a few year later, largely so that the unwanted whey could be fed to the pigs; and small-goods were a natural development. Things were difficult (in contrast with the freezing works) during the second world war, but towards the end of it, in expectation that controls would soon end, a new building and refrigera-tion plant were put up. Controls did not end for nine more years; and it was for this reason that the Yahl company decided to sell the bacon and smallgoods part of the business, keeping the butter and cheese factory.

Under Borthwicks' first managers, F. W. Pengelly and C. J. Woosley, Yahl developed rapidly. During the next few years two chillers were put in; then, an export licence having been granted, the works began to handle a certain amount of beef. Today, though the greater part of its intake con-sists of sheep, the special points about Yahl are, first, the high proportion of pigs that it kills, and, second, its large and increasing local trade; the latter now including hams canned in the works. Its refrigerated vans go as far north as Murray Bridge in South Australia and Hopetoun in Victoria's Mallee district, and north-east to Charlton in the Wimmera district. In coping with the demand for bacon, which has multiplied several times, it is helped by the Portland works: many pigs are killed and frozen there and held until Yahl wants them, and pigs killed at Yahl are sent to Portland for cold storage.

F. W. Pengelly, the first manager, had been in the country and branch department at Audrey House before the war. He was only lent to Australia to help out pending decontrol. When he left Yahl he returned to England and, on the ending of control in 1954, took charge of the branches, depots and country delivery service. Since then he has added to his duties supervision of all the firm's operations in home killed meat in Britain—a growing part of the business today.

The greatest event in that eventful year, 1948, was the purchase of two big cattle stations, Alderley and Stanbroke, in north-western Queensland. These two properties formed part of the Buckingham Downs aggregation, lying a few miles south of Dajarra, which is the head of the railway that runs east through Cloncurry and Charters Towers and serves Bowen. They have a lower rainfall and carry less cattle per square mile than Banchory, but as their combined area is something like 2,000 square miles their total production is considerable. They are used almost entirely for fattening, keeping only a small breeding herd and buying the rest of their complement as steers.

Besides being a useful investment—and another root for Borthwicks in Australian soil—it is a great advantage to the Bowen works to have Alderley and Stanbroke at the other end of some 600 miles of railway. Though so near together, they are distinctly different in character. Stanbroke is typical mineral country (the famous Mount Isa mines are not far to the north). It has a higher average rainfall than Alderley (though still less than Banchory) and abounds in the saline herbage and bushes that are said to give a distinctive flavour to beef.

The round of work at Alderley and Stanbroke is basically the same as at Banchory, or indeed at any cattle station in Queensland. Its pattern is determined by the annual rainfall; for by the time the monsoonal rains arrive, what is left of the pastures have lost their goodness and the cattle begin to lose condition.

From about December to mid-January there are usually thunderstorms. After this some good monsoonal rains can be expected over most of Queensland. By the end of March the rains have stopped and the station springs into activity with the start of the mustering camp. The first thing generally is to round up the whole property and brand calves born during the off season; for with such vast areas it is most economical to leave the bulls with the breeders all the year round. One reason for branding as soon as possible is that—though all Borthwick stations are blessed with honest neighbours—there are unscrupulous characters about who will put their brand on any 'clean skin' they see; so that the manager who keeps well branded up can be sure of a better calving percentage.

The next operation, which is timed in with the branding round, is to draft out the 'fats' and truck them to the works or to market.

A round of Stanbroke normally takes some two to two and a half months; so that, starting at the beginning of April, the trucking stage is reached by about mid-June. During the branding round, fats from outlying parts of the run have been taken to the bullock paddocks where they have been kept for convenience; and these are re-mustered and trucked during June, July and August. By the time this is done there are more calves ready; and so another branding round is made. To finish, it is usual to muster and sort all the horses ready for next year's work.

After this some men—normally ten at Stanbroke—are paid off. But a maintenance team is kept on to attend to the regular servicing of windmills, troughs, fences, etc. The manager and his head stockman have another job to keep them busy—going round to see that the cattle do not die at the bores for lack of water; for at this time of year there can be long periods with no wind to drive the windmills, and when this happens pumping engines have to be got going.

There are two main reasons why stock work is suspended between about the end of October and April. One is heat. The other is that rain, when it comes, makes the ground too boggy for stock movement.

From this digression we must return to our story. There were new departures in fellmongery about this time. Up to now the Portland works had been sending its skins either to the Alma fellmongery at Melbourne—which, as it happened, was owned by the family of James Balderstone, the firm's general manager in Australia—or to Mazamet in France. Now T. B. & S. (France) were getting all the skins they could handle from the Brooklyn works; and skins are more difficult to dry for shipment at Portland, where the air has a higher humidity than that of Melbourne. So Portland was equipped with a fellmongery of its own at a cost of £120,000. A few years later Borthwicks also bought the Alma business from the Balderstone family.

These ventures were not altogether a success. The main reason was economic. Fellmongery costs were much less in France. So when the strong demand from Mazamet resulted in relatively high prices for dried skins, there was a wholesale closing down of fellmongeries in Australia. The Alma business has been disposed of; and the building that was put up as a fell-mongery at Portland is now used for packing dried skins which are shipped to Mazamet as before. Should trading conditions change, it could revert to fellmongery at short notice.

Some experiments that were tried out during these years were not un-connected with the state of the industry in Britain—controls still on meat and free trading only permitted in unrationed 'extras'. At one time it looked as if there were good prospects for the export of poultry from Australia; and Borthwicks bought two poultry works, one in Brisbane and one in Sydney. But the promise did not materialise and both were sold. The firm also ac-quired two butter factories in the south-east of South Australia (part of a great dairy farming district, green as England in its season, where cattle are counted at so many per acre, not per square mile). These too were disposed of. The rabbit business flourished, particularly during the period of meat control, and some of the works, both in Australia and New Zealand, took part in it until it was greatly diminished for a time by myxomatosis in Aus-tralia—a pity for Borthwicks but a great boon to the farmers—and ended completely in New Zealand by an intensive war on rabbits which includes a ban on the sale of their carcases. Both rabbits and the rabbit trade have re-cently revived in Australia.

The local trade did not languish, but, on the contrary, has continued to grow. It received a fillip from the addition of Yahl with its long tradition of service to retailers and excellent reputation over an area which has ex-panded enormously since Borthwicks took it over. In Victoria, in parts of South Australia, in New South Wales (through the firm's office in Sydney) and in Queensland—not, however, in Western Australia—supplies to retail butchers are an increasingly important part of the business. Although within Brisbane itself there is the difficulty, mentioned before, that meat killed at Moreton may not be sold to the public, this can be overcome by using the city's abattoir; and the ban does not apply in the country areas.

In south-west Victoria Borthwicks have some retail shops in such towns as Warrnambool, Hamilton and Casterton, and a chain of shops at Adelaide in South Australia.

The local trade embraces all kinds of meat, though every district has its preference. Its special feature in comparison with the export business con-sists of the bacon, smallgoods and various delicacies which several works now produce in considerable quantities. On the other hand, in Australia particularly, it absorbs an increasing proportion of the meat which would otherwise be exported. The people of any country naturally have first claim on the products of their own land; and this is a service which Borthwicks are glad to give. In addition it benefits the firm's employees by spreading activities, in part at least, over the year. Seasonal employment was taken for granted in the meat works in the old days. It is much less so today.

In New Zealand

In New Zealand too the firm's local trade has grown enormously. One big step in this direction was taken in 1946 when Borthwicks bought the Manawatu Meat and Cold Storage Company, a small but flourishing wholesale and retail business which had then been running for forty years in Palmerston North, about a hundred miles north of Wellington. With it went a subsidiary, the Tiki Bacon Company, with its own bacon curing and small-goods factory.

Joe Curley, who was in New Zealand at the time of the purchase, managed Manawatu for its first year or so with Borthwicks. Some time later the job was taken on by W. E. Shimmin. Bill Shimmin had been with the firm in England before the war, working at Smithfield under R. G. Bremner, at various depots and in Liverpool. After war service with the R.A.S.C. and then a spell with the LWMSA, he volunteered to go to New Zealand. He managed Manawatu for six years. At the end of that time he crossed over to Australia as assistant general manager to Jim Balderstone.

Shimmin's successor as manager at Palmerston North was Peter Norman, son of Ted. He carried on until he had a motor smash, following which he was brought to England to be 'groomed', while completing his recovery, for a more exalted position in New Zealand.

Under the guidance of these and other managers Manawatu and Tiki have developed their trade very considerably. A team of van salesmen covers a wide area. There is a depot in Wellington, and a number of retail shops in both islands, those in South Island being administered for Manawatu by Borthwicks' Christchurch office. Tiki has a second factory in the South Island, attached to the Belfast works, which kills its pigs for it and hands on the carcases for processing into bacon, hams and a variety of delicacies.

Manawatu gets its supplies from all Borthwick works in New Zealand, particularly Feilding and Waingawa, which are nearest to Palmerston North and to Wellington. In serving the public, whether as wholesaler or through its retail shops, it also serves the works (by helping to spread activity over the year) and the farmers (by increasing demand for their livestock). Both Manawatu and Tiki provided a wide range of good things, specially wrapped and packed, to the exploration ship *Endeavour* in preparation for two expeditions to the South Pole. Tiki is developing its export trade to Malaya, New Guinea and other Pacific countries.

The firm also has a wholesale meat business in Northland at Whangarei, 100 miles north of Auckland. Run in harness with its main export business, this local trade enables Borthwicks to buy their farmer clients' stock at all times of the year. Stock is killed at the Whangarei abattoir, and at Moerewa works, which belongs to the Auckland Farmers' Freezing Co-operative.

It has been said that 'outside' works have always played a big part in maintaining Borthwicks' supplies of meat. One of these valuable connections is with the South Otago Freezing Company, a South Island company with its works at Finegand, near Balclutha. What occurred now is best described in that company's own words which were printed in a booklet produced to celebrate its golden jubilee in 1960:

> The directors were of the opinion that they had established themselves in a sound position and were ready to extend their field of operations. It was agreed that steps should be taken to see if it was possible to encourage any one single exporter to take over the whole of the meat, wool and pelts processed at Finegand, so that a sound trading arrangement could be developed with one company rather than the two or three that had been involved for such a long period. In 1948, a fresh agreement with Thos. Borthwick and Sons (A'asia) Ltd. was signed and the agreements of 1932 were terminated. The company was then in the position of dealing with one major exporting firm for the handling of its main exportable items, and at the same time it was launching its development programme which had been delayed for ten years.
>
> The directors had felt for some time that the existing plant was capable of handling a kill of over 400,000 lambs, and it was a delight for the chairman to be able to announce at the end of the 1950 season that this target had been reached. With the introduction of the semi-solo system of killing for a period of three years while the new slaughter-house was being built, this figure of 400,000 sheep and lambs for the season was maintained.

By 1953 the first stage in the development plan had been completed with the opening of the new slaughter-house, and that year the kill passed the 500,000 mark for the first time. Only two years later, in 1955, the 600,000 mark was exceeded and the following season 769,000 sheep and lambs were handled. The fruits of the policy of expansion were now beginning to show themselves to shareholders and farmers in the district.

The booklet adds that this expansion was greatly helped by increased production resulting from the eradication of rabbits, aerial top-dressing of pastures, and the allocation of small holdings to qualified ex-Servicemen. With further development the Finegand works was dealing with more than a million sheep and lambs by 1959.

Such excellent relations with 'outside' works in both countries are an invaluable asset to Borthwicks, particularly as in New Zealand nowadays no private enterprise company is allowed to start new works of its own.

The success story of SOCOLD—as the South Otago company has named itself—continues. It is typical of the advance of the meat industries in Australia and New Zealand since the second world war.

Some Statistical Notes

Albany Works was bought from the West Australian Meat Export Co. Ltd. in 1948 for £A.56,000. The book value today is £A.265,000. The kill today is about 170,000 sheep and lamb and 6,000 cattle: this annual kill needs to improve yet before this venture can be considered wholly successful.

Yahl Works, near Mount Gambier, in South Australia, was bought from the Yahl Co-operative Butter and Cheese Company in 1948 for £A.24,000. £A.150,000 has since been spent. After depreciation, the works stands in the books today at about £A.130,000. Yahl is principally a local trade works.

Rocklea Poultry Works, Brisbane, Queensland, was bought in 1947 for £A.24,000, and, with additions, was sold for £A.35,000 in 1957. **Doonside Poultry Works,** Sydney, N.S.W., was bought for £A.19,000 in 1951, had £A.25,000 spent on it, and was eventually sold for £A.15,500 in 1956. Not a success! Neither was **Penola Butter Factory,** which was bought in 1947 for £A.20,000, had about the same amount spent on it, and was sold in 1956 for £A.25,500.

Manawatu Meat and Cold Storage Company Limited and **Tiki Bacon Company,** bought in 1946 for about £24,000, has since had about £250,000 spent on improvements—to good account. It is mainly a local trade organisation, based in Palmerston North in the North Island of New Zealand, with important branch activities in Wellington and Christchurch.

Borthwick Wharf, Deptford, London

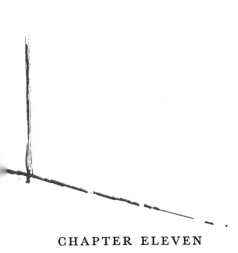
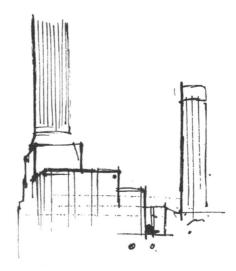

CHAPTER ELEVEN

Free Trading Again

Decontrol came at last in 1954. It had been viewed with some alarm by certain sections of the trade, but in the event the transition to free marketing went unexpectedly easily. There were administrative hurdles, however. Borthwicks' turnover in Britain jumped from about £20,000 (mostly consisting of poultry, rabbits and by-products) in the first week of July 1954, to nearly £324,000 in the second week. The men, though keen, were mostly green either in the handling of meat or in accounting procedures: they depended for guidance on the few who had had experience of the business before September 1939. The senior order clerk at Borthwick Wharf worked from about seven in the morning to eleven at night for six weeks without a single day off.

It took some time for the meat trade to get back to full free enterprise working. There were still big stocks owned by the Government and held by the control organisations. These were worked off gradually. Allotments were made to importers on a percentage basis—three weeks' supply to start with, after which there were weekly meetings between the trade and the Ministry to review quantities and adjust prices. This went on for several months. Meanwhile the first free cargoes of meat began to come in from Australia, New Zealand and the Argentine, including once more chilled beef. There was a time when the two systems, controlled and free, overlapped.

There were other problems. For fifteen years Australia and New Zealand had been selling their meat to the British Government at fixed prices. Now the laws of supply and demand brought about a considerable sorting-out of values. Some prices went up and some went down. In general, meat was still short and very dear. But as time went on the trade adjusted itself and returned to normal; though prices remained several times more than pre-war, largely due to the changed value of money.

To say that the trade returned to normal does not of course mean that it settled down to a steady monotony, a mere projection of old graphs. Far from it.

It is not easy to talk of the trends of these last nine years. History in due time will write down the whole story: then, no doubt, conclusions will seem obvious and we shall pass our judgments accordingly. Meanwhile we can only watch, wait, and reckon as best we may.

An instance that will come to mind is the Common Market. Will Britain ever become a full member of the European Economic Community? Their interests clash in that European countries are so engrossed in raising their own standards of living that they are not prepared to espouse an outward-looking policy towards under-developed countries. Many of these are—or were—British Colonies and countries to which the Commonwealth has accorded membership.

One thing can be said without qualification. Just as Britain has a deep, instinctive feeling, which neither reasoning nor self-interest can touch, for the British Commonwealth, so the great Dominions on their side have shown a remarkable sympathy—instinctive again, unaffected by understanding or misunderstanding of the issue involved—for Britain throughout the deliberations on the Common Market. This is not always apparent in the pronouncements of politicians; but when you talk to the people, particularly those who have some stake in the outcome, it is often astonishing.

Another point can be stated because it is a known fact. The meat industries of Australia and New Zealand have been taking steps—very wise and practicable steps, Common Market or no—to find and cultivate new outlets for their increasing production. Representatives have combed the countries bordering the Pacific and have gone much farther afield. They have had substantial successes. And they are still at work. In New Zealand a special organisation—the New Zealand Meat Export Development Company—was formed to support and encourage the drive.

Instances will appear when we come to outline Borthwicks' activities during these years. One story demands special mention now because it is both important and rather surprising. We tend to think of the United States of America as rich in all natural products and self-supporting (though in fact that insatiable country imports many things, including one of its own best-known indigenous products, petroleum). Certainly so in beef. The cattle ranches of Texas and Arizona are familiar at least to all who patronise the cinema. Yet today America is a major beef customer of Australia and New Zealand (and there are hopes, in New Zealand particularly, that the same may also apply to lamb one day).

What happened was this. Prolonged droughts in the American beef states during the early fifties cut the cattle population down seriously. It took some years to recover. Meanwhile the shortage was made up by importing—from New Zealand first, in 1957, then from Australia also. Australia's exports of beef and mutton to the United States were 7,000 tons odd in 1958, more than 60,000 tons in 1959. In 1961 and 1962 they exceeded by a wide margin her exports to Britain.

American production climbed back to normal in time; but imports did not cease. The needs of the human population (which rose from 157 to 187 million in the last ten years) kept ahead of home supplies. Also—and more important—there was a difference in quality. The Texas farmer takes pride in his 'prime' beef. His cattle are grain fed and their flesh has fat running all through it (this is called marbling in the butcher's shop). The farmer's pride is justified. But the American citizen for some purposes likes his meat lean: and lean meat was what Australia and New Zealand could best supply. Further, lean meat is essential for manufacture of the hamburger, which is virtually a staple food in the States. (The hamburger contains a big percentage of fat: but fat is a surplus product of American cattle. More lean is needed to make up the balance.) It happened that about this time the American Government brought in a school meals programme which enormously increased the demand for hamburgers and similar creations.

So Australia and New Zealand are still sending beef, and some mutton too, to the United States. In the main this is what is called 'manufacturing' quality: that is, it is lean. In the early years of the shortage America took some prime beef 'bone in', in quarters. Now it is almost all boned and packed in cartons. It is used mostly for prepared meats and for the 'institutional' trade (hospitals, railways and restaurants).

The demand from the United States has grown to such proportions that it has siphoned off most of the supplies that used to come to Britain; where the deficit is being made up by the increased production of British farmers, and by larger imports from other countries, notably Yugoslavia.

Providence gives gifts but usually exacts something in return. The American importers' demands are extraordinarily strict. All shipments are inspected on arrival and the least detectable flaw may lead to the rejection of a whole consignment. At the producing end there is a special routine in the works. The meat—lean only—is cut off the bone, packed carefully in cartons, weighed and sealed before freezing.

We shall see more of these special measures in the works later in this chapter. Meanwhile it should be said that the demands of the American market have been a tonic to the industry in Australia and New Zealand. Other points apart, a new standard of hygiene has been set. From this all consumers benefit.

Farmers in both countries are no doubt praying that the human population of the United States may continue to increase faster than the cattle, and that more and more American teenagers may acquire the taste for hamburgers. And perhaps Australians now see at least one reason to be thankful for the dryness of their climate which tends to produce lean beasts.

Both countries have been taking all possible steps to expand and improve their production of meat—which, with its by-products, is New Zealand's biggest earner in the export markets, and in Australia takes third place after wool and wheat. (It is only recently, in fact, that wheat has earned more than meat.) Scientific breeding, land development, irrigation, fertilisers, cattle roads in the Australian outback, transport arrangements and special vehicles—all have been given much thought by farmers, stock and station agents and Governments. Perhaps the most interesting modern technique (it has been mentioned already) is aerial top-dressing. Of nine million acres top-dressed in New Zealand in 1959, three and a half million were treated by aeroplanes. The Dominions and the stock-raising industry move with the times.

Man progresses: but nature and accident still oppose him. This not only in the great open spaces where nature's power is yet uncontrolled—though further examples from Australia are to come—but even in London. On the 23rd January 1958 fire broke out in Smithfield. It was caused by some electrical fault. The firemen were confused by the maze of underground passages and freezing chambers now filled with smoke. Two of them lost their way: their oxygen gave out and they were dead when found.

After twenty-four hours the poultry market was burnt out. Borthwicks lost one stall, No. 264, and a certain amount of meat. The old Cock tavern too was destroyed. Rebuilding, with improvements, took about three years. Thirty skeletons were found buried among the ruins. They might have been the remains of Protestant martyrs who were burned for their faith in the time of Queen Mary.

Borthwicks in Britain

A small but faithful band of 'caretakers' had coped with war-time problems at Audrey House and Colwyn Bay. It had been gradually re-inforced by those who returned during the following difficult period of continued controls. Now it had to face another set of problems and adjust-ments—those involved in the return to free enterprise working. It was fifteen years since any of its members had had actual experience of this. And of course they were all that much older: the average age of those who remained of the 'caretakers' was fifty-two.

Fortunately more reinforcements arrived. R. G. Bremner had found his war-time work with MINDAL exhausting. Often at that time he was so weary for lack of sleep that he could not write or even think clearly. At times he must have looked forward to retirement when peace should come. But as each year passed and it seemed that controls must end soon, he decided to carry on a little longer. When controls did end, he felt bound to see the machinery of free trading established again and working smoothly. He came back to Borthwicks and took sole control, assisted by Joe Curley, of the firm's meat operations through the trying years that followed. He did not retire until December 1959, when the Imported Meat Trade Associa-tion gave a luncheon in his honour. Curley, who had become a director in 1954, succeeded him as a matter of course.

Another of those who came back about the same time as Bremner was William Miles. He then became office manager—a new appointment—under the secretary McCrae. He had had plenty of experience of this kind of work with LWMSA, besides having been right through the Audrey House office from junior clerk upwards, and also, when working on the administra-tive side of the country and branch department in Savage's time, having travelled all round the branches. He retired at the same time as Bremner.

McCrae himself had retired before that—in 1956—owing to ill health. His successor was Gerald Moore—Captain Moore, C.B.E., R.N. He had come to Borthwicks on his retirement from the Navy the year before as staff manager and assistant secretary. His early life, after Osborne and Dartmouth, had been spent at sea. The fact that he was able to take on McCrae's job—and held it so successfully—disposes of the legend that finance is a mystery reserved for regular initiates. Perhaps his staff experience (he was on the personal staff of Admiral Sir Bertram Ramsay, Allied Commander-in-Chief, Expeditionary Force for the Invasion of Europe) has something to do with it. Moore went to Australia and New Zealand the year after his appointment as secretary; he became a director of Borthwicks in 1959, and managing director in 1963.

The return to free trading in meat did not pass without rejoicing. The following letter, dated the 7th October 1954, is addressed from Borthwicks, Audrey House, to William Donald, C.B.E., chairman of the Port Line.

'PORT VINDEX'

Dear Sir,

We feel that the above shipment of free meat—our first since control virtually put an end some fifteen years ago to our long association with the Port Line—is an occasion which ought not to pass unnoticed, and we would like to convey to you and your colleagues our thanks for your active co-operation, and our congratulations on the success of their efforts.

It is an added cause for mutual satisfaction, as we were together in the inauguration of the Chilled Beef Trade from New Zealand, that we again share the distinction of being first to weigh anchor.

The reply, dated the following day, is signed by the deputy chairman of the Port Line:

Dear Sir,

Our Chairman is at present away on leave and so the undersigned is acknowledging your letter of the 7th October. We much appreciate the kind terms in which you have phrased this letter to us on the occasion of the arrival of our 'PORT VINDEX' with the first shipment of free meat by yourselves since the beginning of control fifteen years ago.

Like yourselves, we are very pleased that private enterprise has again become possible, and with you we look forward to many years of that happy association which your Firm and ours have always so much enjoyed and appreciated.

The directors and staff of Borthwicks began doing everything they could to increase the sales of Australian and New Zealand meat not only in Britain but in many other countries. They made numerous visits to America, coming back well primed with the hamburger's status in the American scale of values. But there had been considerable developments before that. The firm had been appointed agents in the United States for the New Zealand Meat Export Development Company. (Having viewed the inception of this body with certain misgivings, once it was in existence the directors decided to support it all they could and to leave nothing undone that could show their willingness to help in the drive for world markets.)

Further, a new company, T. B. & S. (U.S.A.) Limited, was formed in 1960. This was not altogether a new venture but rather a logical development. T. B. & S. (New York) had existed through the thirties, selling meat—including boneless beef—and pelts on commission; and after that the firm was represented in New York by an agent, Mr Benjamin. Later the meat agency went to the Atalanta Trading Corporation, while Antony Gibbs & Co., Inc., of Broadway, handled the sale of pelts and looked after Borthwicks' administrative affairs in America. The new company—which is a wholly owned subsidiary incorporated in the United Kingdom—appointed Antony Gibbs & Co. its secretaries for North America and opened an office at 61 Broadway, across the passage from them. Arthur Hartog, previously manager of Atalanta, became the first manager of T. B. & S. (U.S.A.). Later Gibbs's pelt salesman in Boston, Roger Conant jr., who already regarded himself as a Borthwick man, transferred to the new company, which thus started with men whom it knew and trusted, and who had experience of the firm's business—both in meat and pelts—in the States. So the American company has stepped off on the right foot. Now the firm joins its prayers to those of Australian and New Zealand farmers.

In other countries too there have been developments. The firm has appointed agents in the British West Indies and the Mediterranean since the second world war, and has enormously increased its overseas trade in general during the past five years. (Exports to the West Indies, for instance, jumped from 350 to nearly 2,000 tons in one year.) More on this subject when we make our next and last trip to the Southern Hemisphere and review activities there over the closing period of our story.

The selling organisation has not only expanded into many countries where it did not function before the war; it has also taken on a new character to meet new conditions. It has become expert in exchange regulations and in the various requirements imposed by Governments—British, Dominion and foreign—on the export and import of meat, wool, pelts, and all the multifarious by-products of the meat industry. Representatives are ready to leave for any foreign country at short notice and to battle with the language problem, foreign banks, and the thousand and one officials, any one of whom may be the only person authorised to issue a permit. Incidentally it is surprising how many languages are spoken—some fluently, some well enough to get by—by people in and around head office. (Salesmen are expected to command at least one foreign language; and this qualification will become still more necessary if Britain strengthens her association with Europe.) There is information here about controls, exchange, shipping, transhipment, insurance, payment, licences, and all the hurdles that have to be cleared before an order is taken, goods delivered and money received.

And, with business extending in so many directions, ever-increasing importance devolves on market intelligence. Statistics and more statistics are collected, sorted and filed under the canny direction of Alec Fyffe.

Pastures new

Now we come to a very recent change: a change which is a departure from the whole course of our story up to now, and another instance of how decisions are often no more nor less than an answer to events. Borthwicks in Britain are in the home-killed meat business.

The handling of fresh meat has always been a mystery apart; and Borthwicks, absorbed in their chosen task of selling more and more Australian and New Zealand frozen meat, had felt no urge to seek pastures new. But within the last few years the drive for fresh export markets—in which the firm played its full part—has been so successful that the quantities—in beef particularly—coming to Britain began to fall off noticeably: so much so that the whole sales organisation was in real danger of having less than enough meat to keep it busy and its customers satisfied.

There were other reasons too why the future of supplies from Australia and New Zealand was somewhat doubtful. One was the general uncertainty about imports while the outcome of negotiations with the Common Market was as yet in the balance. Another was the attitude of a number of New Zealand farmers, who were criticising the proportion of their meat that was being handled by 'overseas' companies.

In fact it was becoming urgently necessary, if the depots and market stalls were to be assured of sufficient quantities to sell—and if the selling cost of Australian and New Zealand mutton and lamb in Britain (still, after all, the most important item) was to be prevented from rising—to seek some source of additional supplies. British farmers were increasing their production fast. Here was one obvious answer.

The firm's first step into this field was a minority investment in a new company, Irish Beef Limited, with a works at Dundalk, whose exports to the United Kingdom are handled by Borthwicks. The second was the building, on Borthwicks' own account, of an abattoir at Ross-on-Wye, in Herefordshire: this came into operation in January 1963. The next, a majority shareholding in an abattoir to be built thirty or forty miles south of Edinburgh: various sites are under discussion, but at the time of writing it looks as if the one chosen will be at Galashiels. A small abattoir was also acquired in 1963 at Wisbech in Cambridgeshire.

Further investments in abattoir companies, with Borthwicks handling their output, will probably follow. The firm has already recruited men skilled in the mysteries of home-killed meat and, most important, the staffs at the depots and market stalls have set about adapting themselves with a will to the new techniques.

At the same time the firm has been making arrangements to sell Argentine, Irish, Yugoslav and English meat on commission.

The decision once made to embark on a big new enterprise, it is being tackled by all in the same spirit that animated Thomas Borthwick and his men when they grasped the opportunities of imported frozen meat. Joe Curley, with Frank Pengelly, is in charge.

At Borthwick Wharf

At the time of decontrol an unexpected opportunity came to appoint a new manager at Borthwick Wharf. It was an unusual appointment. Borthwicks were particularly concerned about the bad state of labour relations generally on the Thames; and so they looked for a proved leader first and foremost. Knowledge of the technicalities was secondary: men like Percy Pilch, chief clerk at the Wharf (he has died since, much regretted) and 'Bezzy' Beswarick, senior foreman—first-class men with a lifetime's experience of cold storage—could be trusted to see him through.

The choice fell on Captain H. G. Dickinson, D.S.C., R.N., whose recent service included command of an aircraft carrier and a spell in charge of

Hong Kong dockyard. He became manager of Borthwick Wharf in 1954.

The effect was electric. 'The Captain' commanded his men's respect from the start. And their trust—with good reason; though at Audrey House it was whispered that he was 'the best shop steward the men ever had'. He fought some battles with head office; and in one moment of exasperation he was heard to shout: 'Call my barge alongside.'

But Thames-side life is no picnic even for a hardened deep sea sailor; and one evening in January 1960 'the Captain' died in his chair at home of a heart attack. He had given all he had. And he had done a fine job.

By good luck and good management another naval man, Commander Peter Worth, D.S.C., had joined the firm a year before to be groomed for the succession. He had been posted to Liverpool for experience. He came down at once and took over at the Wharf. Much younger, and toughened by life as a destroyer captain, he was the right man to succeed Dickinson. And he had the sailor's bent for detailed organisation and order. He is there today. His main task now is to re-cast and adjust the complicated routine of Borthwick Wharf to the changing demands of the market and the salesmen. It is making promising progress.

One unique and exacting part of this routine is what is called the 'country delivery service' to butchers. It operates both from Borthwick Wharf and from the Lancashire Cold Store in Liverpool. So far as London is concerned a price list* is sent out weekly to over 2,500 butchers within a radius of 75 miles: it covers every sort and quality, and even every cut, of imported meats, offals, canned meats, rabbits, etc. Travellers follow up and take orders. At the Wharf there are two peak delivery nights each week— Sunday and Wednesday. On Sundays anything up to ninety insulated lorries, capacity four tons each, roll out between midnight and eight in the morning and away in all directions.

The high-speed loading of these lorries is a miracle of organisation. The hundreds of orders, each of which may include quite a variety of items, must be made up with great care. Then they have to be put on the right lorry in the right sequence—in reverse, so to speak—to be ready to come off as the vehicle makes its round. And all against the clock.

Butchers make good use of the country delivery service. And the worse the weather the more they use it. It is a welcome alternative to making their own way through snow and ice to markets or depots. When the pace

*An example of a price list is reproduced between pages 184 and 185.

Top-dressing hill country by light aircraft has been responsible, more than any other single factor, for the vastly increased carrying capacity and productivity of New Zealand since the war. The loading device on the truck will fill the aircraft's hopper within a few seconds of landing

Grading and weighing lambs in a New Zealand works
A boning and cutting room, Brooklyn Works, Melbourne. At the time this photograph was taken the men were preparing meat under contract for the Olympic Games authorities in 1956.

By-products in a New Zealand works. Above: A hide stack. Below: Grading pelts

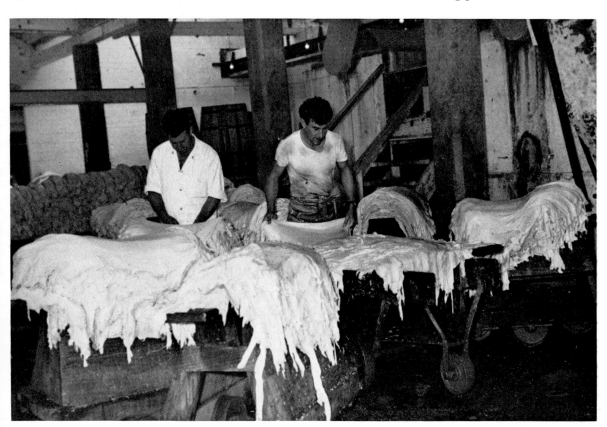

These four pictures show clearly the bustle, the heat, sweat and hard work of a Queensland beef slaughterhouse—and the skill and fitness necessary for most of the work there

173

Trucks and trailers assembled to form a 'road train' in Queensland. As roads improve, these road trains are becoming increasingly used for stock movement

174

Branding cattle on a Western Australian station

Mustering sheep for shearing on a station in New South Wales, Australia

is hottest Borthwicks regularly supplement their own transport by hiring from Monro Transport Limited, whose drivers are as much part of the team as the firm's own men.

The trend at Borthwick Wharf has been towards more and more small orders, more cutting, sorting, wrapping, and packing. The amount of 'fiddly work' to achieve the same tonnage of despatch has increased enormously of recent years. So much so that it began to affect the whole economy of Borthwick Wharf. 'Fiddly work' is no proper job for the hefty dockers who do the loading; nor is it allowed for in their conditions of employment. It was uneconomic use of manpower. And you have to use men, time and everything else efficiently when you are running a 5,000-ton cold store with an average wage, for manual workers, of £23 a week.

The solution was to move as much of this work as could be moved away from the Wharf. In 1960 an arrangement was made with Caleb Lee & Sons, of Swanley, Kent—only 14 miles from Borthwick Wharf—who undertook to cut up a minimum of 50 tons of meat per week. This has cleared the pipeline. The flow is greater than ever.

Improvements go on. The year 1962 saw the first refrigerated barge on the Thames. From the beginning meat had been carried from ship to riverside cold store in insulated barges—operated, in the case of Borthwicks, by Perkins & Homer, later absorbed by the Thames Steam Tug and Lighterage Company. This was fine, except in hot weather when too many frozen lambs go 'soft' with consequent loss in 'bloom' and condition—and value. The solution, a refrigerated barge, had so far been considered by everybody too expensive; but when an engineer, C. N. Blakey, produced a workable design and Covington (Contractors) Limited offered to build a refrigerated fleet at favourable operating rates for the 35,000 tons or so carried by barge every year, the firm gladly encouraged their enterprise. A bonus point for Borthwick Wharf is that, if it is full to capacity, refrigerated barges can be held alongside until the pressure is off instead of being forced to divert the barges and rent cold storage space from someone else.

The travellers work long hours, making thirty to forty calls in a day. Urgent orders are posted in special red envelopes which a messenger collects from the General Post Office after midnight and takes to Borthwick Wharf. Others are put through by telephone. The scene at the Wharf is full of streamlined activity—opening the red envelopes; taking calls on an array of telephones, each distinctively coloured to avoid confusion; vast volumes of paper work helped by calculating machines; detailed instructions for the making up of individual orders to be loaded on to the waiting delivery vans.

The van-drivers are the butchers' friends. Often they are entrusted with the key of the shop so that when the butcher comes in in the morning he finds his meat already neatly stowed in the refrigerator.

The system is essentially the same at the 3,000-ton Lancashire Cold Store. Then there are the market stalls and smaller depots at strategic points spread all over the country. The whole organisation is the result of a hundred years of experience, plus endless hard work every day and night— much of it done when most of us are asleep in our beds.

Growth and change

By-products are a subject on their own. Even if it were not a peculiarly interesting subject it would have to be studied; because by-products play an essential part in the economics of meat. But it *is* an interesting subject, leading into all sorts of unexpected by-ways and unfamiliar industries. Did you know, for instance, that stearine from animal fat goes into some kinds of sweets? That inedible fats and blood albumen are both used in preparing leather? That ground bone helps to harden steel? That cattle's feet are processed into fine lubricants such as cutting oils, and others that are used in the textile trades? That ground horns and hooves help to maintain the foam produced by fire extinguishers? That 'goldbeater's skin' is part of an animal's guts? Or that Borthwicks supply in an average year enough surgical ligatures—lambs' intestines, selected and prepared—for 685,000 operations to the London Hospital, which in turn exports them to all parts of the world, including New Zealand where they started?

These are some of the less familiar uses of animal by-products. To list the better known would take many pages. There are a great many of them and they are sold in hundreds of different markets. Many of these markets are in Britain. Most of the wool, for instance, goes to Bradford. But some of it goes to America or Europe, as do most pelts; some hides to the Iron Curtain countries and Japan; tallow to Africa and Asia . . . and so on.

Up to 1939 (when most by-products came under control) this highly complicated side of the business had been looked after at Audrey House by two technical experts, both of whom had since died. Now Jason Borthwick took it on with Eric Watson to help him and John Borthwick as his under-study. They reopened old markets and found new ones while they learned from scratch as the various by-products were released from control. Fortunately the latter process was slow and gradual. Meanwhile the job grew under their eyes. So much so that in 1955 the whole department moved into its own office at Bristol House, Holborn Viaduct, a stone's throw from Audrey House. There Watson and his staff carried on for eight years. There are not many of them but they handle biggish business. In an average year they deal with about £4 million worth of sheepskins alone. Some of the smaller items have a high value; for instance various glands which are used medicinally (though nowadays many of these products are being replaced by synthetic substances).

Here are figures of the total f.o.b. values of some typical by-products produced by Borthwicks in Australia and New Zealand in one recent year: wool, £1,850,000; pelts, £1,370,000; skins, £1,320,000; casings, £988,000; hides and calfskins £732,000; tallow (including neatsfoot oil, etc.), £670,000; meals, etc., £347,000; miscellaneous (including such mysterious items as lamb bung caps, vells, gall, tail hair and various glands), £190,000; total for all by-products, nearly £7½ million.

One more change to be written into our story before it goes to press. We have to say goodbye to Audrey House. A sad moment for all who have spent their working lives in it and, if they went away, have always come back to it again. Sad too for those beyond the seas who have come there as a matter of course whenever they visited the old country, and for many more who have regarded it as the heart of Borthwicks all over the world. Indeed it has been so for nearly as long as the oldest of those who are still working can remember. Yet a cheerful moment too, for it is another stage in the process of growth.

The firm's new headquarters, occupied in May 1963, is Priory House, in St John's Lane, near the junction of Farringdon Road and Clerkenwell Road. It is a fine new building with five floors and basement, and Borthwicks have taken the whole of it. It is only a short distance from Audrey House and—there would be something wrong if the firm's headquarters were not—within easy reach of Smithfield. The drawing on page 208 shows, at the left, the Gatehouse of the Grand Priory of the Order of St John of Jerusalem, originally built in 1148 and last reconstructed in 1559.

So the story of Borthwicks in London reaches its end, if end is the right word, with memories of the past, the present new and fresh, and a promise for the future.

In Australia

As we turn to Australia and New Zealand in these challenging years of post-war decontrol we meet once more a problem which has been touched on in the previous chapter—the effects of inflation. Borthwicks now found themselves in exactly the opposite position from that which prevailed after the first world war. Then the prospects of development seemed discouraging, and the firm's reserves were more than adequate. Now, opportunity beckoned on every side; but, though there seemed to be a lot of money waiting to be used, its purchasing power was sadly reduced. The directors were compelled to pick and choose their investments. Inflation, combined with high taxation, definitely acted as a brake on further development.

This notwithstanding, the return of real peace-time conditions was a great occasion. One of the signs was that chilled beef shipments started again. When Bowen loaded its first post-war consignment of chilled beef on to the *Cretic* in September 1955, old hands who had learned the tricks of this trade more than sixteen years ago came along to help and advise. Chilling went ahead for the next few years and then gave place to the export of packaged boneless meat to the United States.

The greatest effort in Australia during these years has been the drive for new overseas markets, not only in America but also in the West Indies, Africa, the Persian Gulf, the Near and Far East and the Pacific Islands. It was a busy time for the Melbourne head office. Both Jim Balderstone and Bill Shimmin, his second-in-command, travelled far and often. Shimmin is no longer in Melbourne: in 1962 he was granted extended long service leave before taking up a new appointment. Duncan McFarlane took on the job of assistant general manager in Australia. Before this he had been deputy manager of the Brisbane branch. It is worth noting that, like those two London directors, Joe Curley and Alec Fyffe, McFarlane also began his life with the firm as an office boy—in Adelaide.

The local trade grows every year. In this Borthwicks are doing their bit towards satisfying a general trend. Today about 80 per cent of Australia's meat production is consumed in the country. This of course does not lessen Australia's determination to sell more overseas. Meat is, as we have said, one of her chief earners in export markets, and in fact her biggest earner of dollar currency, although she is not so dependent on it as New Zealand.

One recent special contract within the country is interesting. In 1956 the Duke of Edinburgh opened the sixteenth Olympiad in the main stadium, the Melbourne cricket ground. The Olympic village at Heidelberg housed some 6,000 athletes and officials. All meat eaten there was supplied by Borthwicks. Four works took part in this operation—Brooklyn, Portland, Moreton and Bowen. Great efforts were made so that nothing but the best should be provided—including, it was estimated, some 30,000 T-bone steaks and 20,000 rump steaks. Particular tastes and religious requirements were allowed for. At Brooklyn Mohammedan priests supervised the killing for Moslem athletes.

Nature continues her efforts to thwart man's progress. Fire broke out at the Portland works early on Christmas morning 1954; but prompt action by the town and works fire brigades prevented serious damage. On the 16th February 1959 Bowen received a visit from Connie. This was not so welcome as might be supposed, for Connie was a cyclone—the second in two years and the worst ever recorded on the east coast of Australia. She battered the town for some thirty hours, with a wind velocity of 116 miles an hour around midnight. Though the works suffered damage amounting to several thousand pounds, the maintenance team got things going again in remarkably short time. The drought of 1957–58 was one of the worst ever in Western Queensland; another in 1960–61 affected a wider area. Such reverses Australians have learned to take in their stride.

Another misfortune, bitterer because it is made by man and apparently irreparable. Banchory, Borthwicks' first cattle station, has been whittled down through the Government's policy of not renewing leases when they expire. The new lease covers only 120 square miles. The rest of the land has been parcelled out to individual farmers ('selectors' in Queensland). Many of these men are ex-service and many of them are good workers; but whether the practice is in the national interest is open to question, particularly where so much depends on having ample money for improvements; and Borthwicks are proud of what they have done for Banchory in the past. In any case it is sad to have to say goodbye to all those square miles that Ted Tooker and Sam and Ken Goodwin and other good men now gone looked after so lovingly for many years.

Sadder still, the old Banchory homestead stands on the lost land. The blow had been foreseen and a new house built for the station manager and his family. It is a modern building with modern comforts, including a much improved water supply from a big dam that was specially constructed. So progress goes on, but with an occasional backward look of regret.

A happy occasion to round off our story of the firm in Australia. In 1955

Portland celebrated its golden jubilee as a Borthwick works. Pat Borth-wick was there from New Zealand, his son Tom, John Borthwick and his wife from London, and Jim Balderstone, general manager in Australia. There were speeches and reminiscences. The Mayor of Portland pointed out that the works wages bill had grown in those fifty years from £68 to a quarter of a million.* Pat Borthwick recalled that his family had been in the meat business since the twelfth century when his ancestors built a castle in Scotland to keep the cattle they 'pinched' from the English; and he read a cable from his brother Algy, the chairman, wishing Portland another bright fifty years.

The proudest man present was the works manager, Hugh Keiller—a Portland man born, schooled in Portland, who started in the Portland works in 1910. When he retired a little later, in 1960, he had served with Borthwicks for fifty years, thirty of them as manager of the Portland works. (He had not spent all his life in his home town: he worked at Brooklyn and in the Melbourne office before he became works manager.) Now he devotes much of his time to the history and natural history of Portland.

After the jubilee and before he retired, Hugh Keiller had seen through two successive extensions which made his beloved Portland the largest country meat works in the southern states.

Tom Borthwick is the eldest and first to be mentioned of the fourth generation. There are three representatives of it in the firm now—all, as it happens, grandsons of Algernon, who was Thomas's youngest son. Christopher Fleming is a son of one of Algernon's daughters. Malcolm Borthwick, Algy's son, has just started his training in Liverpool. Tom, Pat's son, though his father lives in New Zealand and he himself went to school in England and started with the firm at Smithfield, is an Australian by adoption and choice. He has worked in almost every part of the firm's Australian organisation (besides Mazamet and both islands of New Zealand) and has now taken on the much lamented Ken Goodwin's job as pastoral inspector of the Queensland cattle stations. He married an Australian girl from Adelaide, and they live at Frankston, Victoria, where their son Thomas, the first of the fifth generation, is already on the road to manhood.

* This is rather misleading. The figure of £68 was for one month only. For the first whole year the wage bill was £3,410. Since 1955 it has risen to well over half a million.

In New Zealand

Two years after the return to free trading—in 1956—Ted Norman retired, having served twenty-six years as Borthwicks' general manager in New Zealand and for the last eleven years as a director of T. B. & S. (Australasia). The man destined to take his place was his son Peter; who at this time, as has been said, was in England, where he was rapidly establishing himself in the directors' confidence. Meanwhile the job in New Zealand was taken on by Michael Sandwith. Sandwith, after war service in destroyers with the R.N.V.R., had qualified as a chartered accountant, and later joined Borthwicks as assistant to the secretary. He now came out to New Zealand as general manager and a director of T. B. & S. (Australasia). Here he carried on for three years, by which time Peter Norman was ready to take over. Sandwith then came back to England and became a director of the parent company—one of the four present members of the Board (with Joe Curley, A. T. Fyffe and Gerald Moore) not members of the family.

Not long after Michael Sandwith took over as general manager, in 1958, the New Zealand head office was moved again. The migration to the North Island had proved perfectly sound, and Masterton was central, near to Waingawa, and not too far from Feilding and Palmerston North. But the difficulties of administering an expanding business, particularly one concerned with export, from a country town became increasingly evident. Wellington was the obvious place. So to Wellington Borthwicks' New Zealand headquarters went, and took up its abode at 11 Johnston Street, where it remains today. Here it is within a few minutes' walk of the great port, the headquarters of the Meat Board and Government offices.

Peter Norman embarked on his hard job in New Zealand with every advantage. Besides what was in his blood, his own natural gifts, and the confidence of the directors and all who serve under him, he had the moral support and advice of his father, who lived near Masterton within easy reach. Ted knew the answers to most knotty questions that could arise—though of course there are always new ones; and he had not shaken off (how could he?) his interest in the work which he himself did for so many years. In addition Peter has as his second-in-command W. R. Mathieson, an old hand in New Zealand's meat business.

Bill Mathieson is a chartered secretary and a fellow of the New Zealand Society of Accountants. He served with the Meat Board from 1924 to 1939. He was co-author of the Scott-Mathieson report on the meat industry in

1936. In the second world war he was head of the meat division of the export marketing department, which administered the bulk purchase contracts. Joining Borthwicks, New Zealand, in 1946 as secretary, he rose to assistant general manager in 1962. He was chairman of the committee which represented the Freezing Companies' Association at the commission of enquiry into the meat industry in 1959.

Another among the experienced men on whom Peter Norman can rely is F. M. Ollivier, manager of the by-products department. Frank joined Borthwicks in 1945 and specialised in skins and wool. He is on the management committee of the New Zealand Leather and Shoe Research Association and served as its chairman for a term. He is recognised in the industry as an authority on the processing of wool, pelts and hides.

Pat Borthwick too is still resident director and farming in the Wairarapa, and—though he is liable to turn up anywhere in Australia, or for that matter at Priory House, London, at almost any time—is a frequent and very active visitor at the New Zealand head office and the various works. Incidentally there is a story of one of his visits to Feilding. Before starting round the works he went to the store to collect a pair of gum boots. Storeman Hooper had lately been given instructions that the rules about issue of equipment must be strictly enforced. 'Have you got a chit?' he asked. 'No. But . . .' 'Sorry, sir,' said Hooper. 'Orders is orders. No chit, no boots.' 'Quite right,' said the family resident director, and went off to get his chit.

A big drive during these years, in New Zealand as in Australia, has been for new markets overseas. Japan, with its huge population, is one of the most interesting prospects. Trade with this market was opened up in 1957 by Borthwicks selling a 500-ton shipload to an enterprising business man, Mr Shriro, who sent down a whaler to pick it up. This pointed the way, and a steady trade followed, with the 'conference lines' laying on a shipping service for the purpose. The Japanese Government sponsored an 'eat more meat' campaign to increase the protein in the people's diet. Borthwicks responded with a visit by Peter Norman. This was followed up by the sales manager from Wellington, A. L. Paterson; he went to Tokyo to see C. Itoh & Company, one of the country's biggest commercial houses, who were then appointed Borthwicks' agents in Japan for supplies both to the American Army and to domestic consumers.

Demand was slow at the start, but now Japan is buying big quantities of ewe mutton from New Zealand—up to 25,000 tons a year—and will take

THOMAS BORTHWICK & SONS LTD.

HEAD OFFICE:
Priory House, St. John's Lane,
London, E.C.1

BRANCHES:

BATH	LEEDS	PLYMOUTH
BIRMINGHAM	LEICESTER	ROMFORD
BRIGHTON	LIVERPOOL	ROSS-ON-WYE
BRISTOL	LUTON	SOUTHAMPTON
CARDIFF	MANCHESTER	STOKE
CHELTENHAM	NEWCASTLE	SWANSEA
CROYDON	NEWPORT	SWINDON
EDINBURGH	NOTTINGHAM	WALSALL
GLASGOW	PONTYPRIDD	WATFORD
HULL	PORTSMOUTH	WESTON S/M
KINGSTON		WOLVERHAMPTON

CENTRAL MARKETS, LONDON

BORTHWICK WHARF,
BORTHWICK STREET, S.E.8

COLD STORES:
Borthwick Wharf, London, S.E.8
Canada Dock, Liverpool, 20

**COMMONWEALTH OFFICES
& FREEZING WORKS:**

AUSTRALIA
ADELAIDE · ALBANY · BOWEN
BRISBANE · MELBOURNE · PORTLAND

NEW ZEALAND
CANTERBURY · CHRISTCHURCH · FEILDING
WAINGAWA · WAITARA · WELLINGTON

Telegrams: "OVERDRAW, GREEN, LONDON"   Telephone: TIDEWAY 1250 (8 lines)

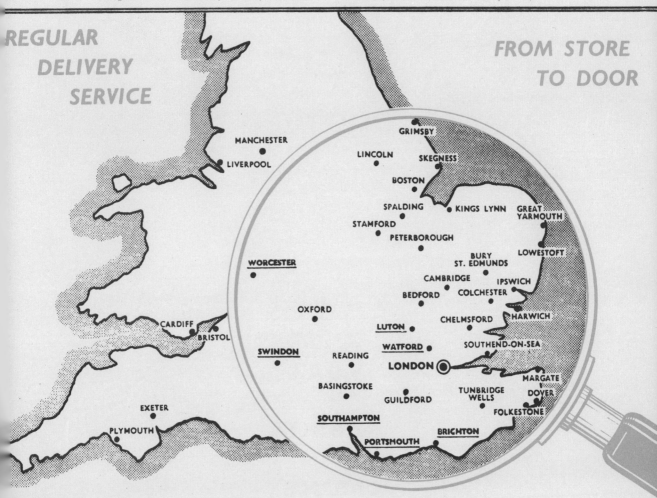

REGULAR DELIVERY SERVICE

FROM STORE TO DOOR

QUOTATIONS FOR WEEK ENDING:—
JANUARY 12th, 1963

SUBJECT TO MARKET FLUCTUATIONS AND SUPPLIES BEING AVAILABLE

LAMB

	Av. Weight about	per lb.
Choice "CHAIN" Brand, New Season	27 lbs.	2/2
" " " " "	32 lbs.	2/1
Selected New Zealand "EGMONT DOWN" Brand, New Season	32 lbs.	2/1
Selected Australian New Season	34 lbs.	1/10
" " " "	39 lbs.	1/7½
" " " "	45 lbs.	1/6½
Good Australian "TALLAROOK" Brand, New Season	32 lbs.	1/9½
Australian "FIR" Brand, New Season	25 lbs.	1/10
Selected New Zealand	32 lbs.	1/10½
" " "	38 lbs.	1/8
" " "	44 lbs.	1/6½
Selected New Zealand Down	27 lbs.	1/11½
Good New Zealand	26 lbs.	1/11½
" " "	31 lbs.	1/10

Cut Lamb

Hindquarters	2/6 per lb.	Legs	2/11 per lb.	Shoulders	1/6
Short Forequarters (Ex Breasts)			1/3 „ „	Chines and Ends	1/11

MUTTON

	Av. Weight about	per lb.
Selected New Zealand HOGGETS	44 lbs.	1/4
" " "	52 lbs.	1/2
Selected New Zealand WETHERS	44 lbs.	1/2½
" " " "	52 lbs.	1/1½
" " " "	60 lbs.	1/1½
" " " "	67 lbs.	11½d.
Good New Zealand WETHERS	42 lbs.	1/1
Prime New Zealand EWES	44 lbs.	11½d.
" " " "	52 lbs.	11¼d.
" " " "	60 lbs.	10½d.
" " " "	67 lbs.	9½d.

Cut Mutton

Wether Legs	2/3 per lb.	Ewe Legs	1/8
Australian Wether Legs under 8 lbs. each (in cases about 90 lbs.)			1/7

VEAL

Australian BONED BOBBY (in cartons about 70 lbs.)	2/6

RABBITS

	Per case
Australian SKINNED 60 lbs. net at 2/11 per lb.	£8.15.0

CASINGS

			Per Bundle
North American Long Hog	24/– per bundle	North American Long Short Hog	16/–
English Long Hog	23/6 „ „	New Zealand No. 1 Chipolata	27/6

BEEF

	EX STORE LONDON Av. Weight about	per lb.
Selected Australian **OX HINDS**	130-150 lbs.	1/9
„ „ „ **CROPS**	110-130 lbs.	1/6
Selected New Zealand **OX HINDS**	130-150 lbs.	1/9
„ „ „ „ **FORES**	130-150 lbs.	1/2
Prime New Zealand **COW HINDS** (Ex Kidney Knob)	120-140 lbs.	1/5
Argentine Chiller Quality **HINDS**	140-160 lbs.	1/9
„ „ „ **FORES**	140-160 lbs.	1/2

Cut Beef

Toppieces	1/9 per lb.	**Rumps**	2/4 per lb.	**Loins**	2/1
Foreribs	1/6 „ „	**Rumps and Loins**	2/1 „ „	**Flanks**	9d.
		Shins/Legs	1/2 „ „		

Boneless Beef

	In cartons			In cartons	
Australian Ox Silversides	80 lbs.	2/10 per lb.	**South African Cape Ox**		
„ „ **Topsides**	60 lbs.	2/10 „ „	**Silversides**	70 lbs.	2/10
„ „ **Rumps**	60 lbs.	2/9 „ „	**Topsides**	70 lbs.	2/10
„ „ **Crops**	80 lbs.	2/3 „ „	**Australian Cow Crops**	70 lbs.	2/2
„ „ **Chucks**	80 lbs.	2/3½ „ „	„ „ **Chucks & Blades**	70 lbs.	2/2½
„ „ **Blades**	80 lbs.	2/3½ „ „			
„ „ **Thick Flanks**	60 lbs.	2/7 „ „			
Shins	60 lbs.	2/4 per lb.			

SUNDRIES

OX CHEEKS	1/1 per lb.	SHEEP TONGUES		1/–
„ SKIRTS	2/2 „ „	„ LIVERS (pails)		3/1
„ TONGUES (Short Cut)	2/– „ „	„ HEARTS		1/8
„ LIVERS	2/– „ „	„ KIDNEYS		2/4
„ TAILS	1/10 „ „	LAMB LIVERS (pails)		3/8
„ KIDNEYS	2/2 „ „	„ HEARTS		2/1
„ BREADS	2/4 „ „	„ BREADS		3/7
„ HEARTS	1/4 „ „	PIG KIDNEYS		2/6
BOBBY CALF TONGUES	1/6 „ „	„ LIVERS		2/5
„ „ HEARTS	1/8 „ „	„ MELTS		1/4
„ „ KIDNEYS	1/9 „ „			
„ „ BREADS	3/7 „ „			

CANNED MEATS

CONTINENTAL

	Per case
HAM (Skinless and Fatless) In cases 24 x 1 lb. at 6/6 per tin (per case)	£7.16.0
HAM (Skinless and Fatless) In cases 24 x 2 lb. at 12/3 per tin (per case)	£14.14.0
HAM (Skinless and Fatless) 6 tins per case, 9/12 lbs. per tin (*charged gross for net*)	5/–
SHOULDERS (Skinless and Fatless) 6 tins per case, 9/12 lbs. per tin (*charged gross for net*)	4/–

	Per case
OX TONGUES In cases 6 x 6 lbs. at 6/5 per lb.	£11.11.0
„ „ „ „ 24 x 1 lb. at 6/11 per tin	£8.6.0
PORK LUNCHEON MEAT In cases 12 x 2 lbs. at 1/11 per lb.	£2.6.0
PORK & BEEF LUNCHEON MEAT In cases 24 x 7 ozs. at 1/3 per tin	£1.10.0

AUSTRALIAN

CORNED BEEF In cases 12 x 6 lbs. at 2/10 per lb.	£10.4.0

SOUTH AMERICAN

CORNED BEEF In cases 6 x 4 at 3/4 per lb.	£4.0.0
„ „ „ „ 48 x 7 ozs. at 2/1 per tin	£5.0.0

r Forms, which are supplied on application.

not undertake the Special Night Delivery Service arranged for them.

bags when returned in good condition, consigned "CARRIAGE PAID HOME," within 14 days to

SELECTED FRESH KILLED MEAT

Beef

EX SMITHFIELD MARKET

	Average Weight about	per lb.
HINDS	150 lbs.	At Market Price
,,	180 lbs.	,,
,,	200 lbs.	,,
FORES	150 lbs.	,,
,,	180 lbs.	,,
,,	200 lbs.	,,
SHORT FORES		,,
TOPPIECES		,,
RUMPS AND LOINS Ex Flank		,,
,, ,, ,, ,, ,, Ex Kidney Knob		,,
RUMPS		,,
LOINS Ex Flank		,,
,, ,, ,, Ex Kidney Knob		,,
FORERIBS		,,
FLANKS		,,
KIDNEY KNOBS		,,

Lamb

LAMB	35 lbs.	At Market Price
,,	40 lbs.	,,
,,	50 lbs.	,,
HINDQUARTERS		,,
LEGS	over 5 lbs.	,,
SHOULDERS	over 5 lbs.	,,
HINDS AND ENDS		,,
CHINES AND ENDS		,,

Pork

PIGS	60-80 lbs.	At Market Price
,,	80-100 lbs.	,,
,,	100-120 lbs.	,,
,,	140-160 lbs.	,,
BELLIES	At Market Price	LONG LOINS	,,
HANDS	,,	LONG HOGMEATS	,,
LEGS 14 lbs. and over	,,	HANDS AND BELLIES	,,

Veal

DUTCH CALVES	160-180 lbs.	At Market Price
CALVES	60 lbs.	,,
,,	80 lbs.	,,
,,	100 lbs.	,,
,, Bobby	40 lbs.	,,
PAIRS HINDS 25 lbs. At Market Price PAIRS FORES	25 lbs.	,,

OFFALS, etc. We can supply at Market Prices

CONDITIONS OF SALE

Above goods sold by us are, to the best of our knowledge. sound and free from disease. but no Warranty to that effect is given or can be implied.

NO CLAIM ALLOWED UNLESS NOTIFIED ON DAY OF RECEIPT

NOTE.—Orders for Town Killed Meat are executed by Rail or Local Carrier.

more as the people's—particularly the children's—taste turns in favour of the hitherto unfamiliar fare.

Peter Norman was in America and the West Indies in 1961, returning through California, Honolulu and Fiji. Altogether Borthwicks, New Zealand, are today exporting meat to some forty countries. The search for new markets is shared by all companies: more than one-third of all meat exported from New Zealand now goes to markets other than Britain. In 1939 only one-half of one per cent went to other markets.

The local trade continues to grow, though it has not reached quite the same proportions as in Australia. It does not affect export to Britain—still easily the country's biggest customer—partly because New Zealanders, who supply the world with lamb, do not eat much of it themselves: they prefer hogget (yearling lamb).

There have been more improvements at all the works. The most spectacular was another unorthodox piece of engineering carried out at Waitara —which had already seen so many reconstructions and extensions in its fifty-two years as a Borthwick works—at the very beginning of this period, in 1954. The Waitara cold store was very old and its size quite inadequate for present demands. The works area is bounded on one side by the river and on the other side by the town, so that the only possible direction in which to extend was upwards. The store, being so old and built of wood, could not carry another storey on top of its existing two. On the other hand it was too valuable to be dismantled and replaced. What was to be done? There was only one answer—lift the existing two storeys and build another underneath them. This was done. And it was done between killing seasons, so that the store was never out of action when it was wanted.

The operation was planned by Ian Macallan, A.M.I.C.E., A.M.N.Z.E., of Wellington, and supervised by the firm's own engineer, Ted Blacker. Special jacks, designed and manufactured in New Zealand, inched up the building a total of $11\frac{1}{2}$ feet, in two sections, each half an acre in area and weighing 4,000 tons. Then it was put back into use while excavation and construction went on below. The final result was 450,000 cubic feet of additional refrigerated space and 250,000 cubic feet of general storage in the basement. Excavation amounted to 15,000 tons; the spoil was used to make up 300 yards of the river bank. If anyone has an appetite for more figures, 8,000 tons of concrete, eight miles of refrigeration piping and three and a half acres of three-inch corkboard were used in the new construction.

Development of the works means a great deal more than new or improved buildings. It also means new or improved machinery, equipment and techniques. In both countries this subject is often in the minds of directors and general managers, never out of the minds of specialist engineers. New Zealand takes particular pride in its development workshop, which is attached to the Waingawa works. It has its own trained men and is under the wing of Ted Blacker, the superintending engineer in Wellington.

Every works, of course, has its own maintenance staff. In the Waingawa workshops you find the back-room boys of the business. They pick up half-formed ideas—whether from Borthwick men or from outside sources—try them out in practice and, if they prove workable, devise the requisite machines. They build pilot plants and often construct the final equipment; though special parts and, where necessary, complete machines are manufactured to their designs by New Zealand firms. Also, having the facilities, they turn out various gadgets that are in constant demand by the works —mutton slides by the thousand, gambrels, band saws for carcase cutting.

But it is the innovations born in the workshop that are the real reason for its existence. Examples will show both the range of work done here and the multifarious problems that arise in a meat works. One, which first took shape at Waingawa ten years ago (the basic idea came from an 'outside' works, Whakatu) and can now be seen in almost any works in Australia or New Zealand, is the Slipemaster. 'Slipe' wool is wool that is removed from the dead skin, not shorn from the living sheep. At one time skin trimmings were thrown outside for nature to work on them. The skin rotted or was eaten away, after which the wool was gathered from the unsavoury pile by 'pie-pickers'. The Slipemaster has earned blessings not only from the trade— it saves time and gives better conditioned wool—but also from the pie-pickers' friends and relations; for they carried their distinctive aroma with them permanently and nothing could remove it.

Freezing could hardly escape these back-room boys' attentions. One method, which they developed in collaboration with a New Zealand engineering firm, can freeze a lamb carcase, once a four days' job, over-night. It is now being worked on by the Meat Industries Research Institute for the benefit of all. Another, thrashed out here and first operated at the Feilding works, applies blast freezing techniques both to carcases and car-tons, and makes an important contribution to the new American trade.

There are plenty more ideas either already working or being worked on —a wool drier that does the job in less time, at less cost, and occupies a quarter of the space; a continuous multi-tube blood drier; a trotter skinner that saves the wool from the bottom joint of the leg and gives a higher yield of neatsfoot oil; a rapid tallow cooler. These and other inventions pioneered at Waingawa represent a substantial yield on the money and effort invested: they are helping, or soon will help, to cut down production costs not only in the Borthwick works but throughout the industry. The development workshop has its programme planned five years ahead. It also provides a training ground for engineering apprentices who go out to all the works.

Waingawa is worth a special look for several reasons. It is the one place in New Zealand where Borthwicks have gone in for stock raising. This is an experiment and on a small scale. The Waingawa farm covers only about 250 acres. It is criss-crossed by a regular pattern of gated dykes like a Wiltshire water meadow. The sections are flooded in rotation with water which, coming from the works where large quantities are used in all departments for cleansing, carries a high content of animal matter. The aim is to test the effects of irrigating pastures with this effluent. At times the farm carries up to 8,000 wethers, which of course finish up in the works. No conclusions will be drawn until further trials have been made. Here too, as at all the firm's New Zealand works, you can see coopers at work making the wooden casks of various sizes and shapes in which tallow, pelts and casings are packed for export. Casks for casings—the valuable intestines, different parts of which will become tennis racket strings, sausage skins and surgical ligatures—are made of imported American oak. Here is a laboratory which, besides carrying out the normal routine tests on all meat and by-products, is engaged on research. In this it collaborates with a sister laboratory at Feilding. The two together have, in the sphere of chemistry, the same function as the Waingawa workshop in engineering—development. It is in places like these that improvements and economies which may affect the future of the whole meat industry are worked out.

Ted Norman

While this book was being prepared for the press, sad news came from New Zealand. Ted Norman died at Masterton on the 8th March, 1963. He had served the firm for forty-five years, for the last twenty-six years as general manager in New Zealand; and since he retired seven years ago had always kept in close touch. Though deeply mourned, he will not be forgotten. It is a happy thought that his son now holds the same position just as James Balderstone's son does in Australia.

In both countries

Wherever you go, in Australia or New Zealand, you can see that big changes have come to the meat industry in these last nine years. In the cold stores at any works are endless lines of sheep and lamb carcases and beef quarters: this is as before, though today many more are destined for countries other than Britain. But you will also see thousands of cartons; and these are something new. They are neatly packed with lean meat cut from the bone—no fat and no gristle. They are probably bound for America; though this is not certain, for nowadays they may go to supermarkets in Britain, or perhaps to some other country. Boneless meat, a big thing today, has a bigger future.

The cartons, solidly packed with meat and no waste, are easy to handle; they save shipping space and freight costs. But their freezing presented some problems. Here the recently developed blast freezing techniques have proved invaluable.

Boneless meat also, of course, requires extra labour and care in its preparation: a great deal of extra labour and care to meet the exacting demands of the American market. The boning tables have non-chip tops made of special composition. The cut meat travels on conveyor belts that are endlessly washed by continuous water jets. The rooms are fitted with fly screens and smoke-excluding devices. The inspectors are hawk-eyed. Countless precautions. . . . But this is what America wants; and America pays; and American orders are worth having. And there are other markets. And in any case the shake-up has done us all good.

Standards have gone up all round; and the employees have benefited as much as anyone. Consider today's rates of pay and working conditions, and the contributory pension scheme that guarantees all Borthwicks' permanent staff security and comfortable retirement. Look at the works gardens—a blaze of colour in the sunshine, the special pride of some devoted Adam. When a gardener's job at one of the works is advertised there is never a lack of applicants.

Because the number of Borthwick employees is so large and they are scattered over such great distances, they have their own news magazines— the *Diamond* in Australia, the *Bulletin* in New Zealand—to keep the big family together, to tell them of each other's achievements in work and play; who has got married, who has achieved a son or a daughter to be the fourth generation employed in the firm, and who has received the coveted

Smithfield

gold watch; and to give them interesting facts about the history of the trade, its present position and future prospects.

The firm has many relationships which are vital to it. The relationship with its own workpeople is most important of all. Next come its clients, the farmers; and they too see the *Diamond* or the *Bulletin*, which often carry paragraphs of special interest to them. Then there are the various Government departments and the Meat Boards. Their co-operation is essential. They are almost always friendly and helpful; for, though there may be differences, basic interests are after all the same.

A special place among these relationships is held by the shipping lines, without whom there would be no meat export trade. There was a time when services were mutual: Borthwicks acted as the shipping companies' agents at certain ports, arranging cargo shipments, dock labour, pilotage, customs clearance and other necessaries. Hugh Keiller remembers those days at Portland—and particularly those nights, not infrequent, when he had to go out in a boat and up the Jacob's ladder to take a stowaway off an outward-bound vessel. Now, with few exceptions, such arrangements are no more. But the shipping lines are carrying more meat every year to more and more destinations. There is continual pressure on them, as on the meat companies, to keep their equipment and services in line with today's requirements.

The firm's business grows in complexity as (with new markets, new agencies and the American company) the distances to be covered increase. It owes a big debt to modern communications, which keep London in quick touch with Melbourne and Wellington, Melbourne and Wellington with the works and the buying organisations. How long did Thomas Banks Borthwick spend on the boat between England and Australia? His eventful crossing to New Zealand has been described. Today you can lunch in Sydney one day and in London the next (the *Comet* takes thirty-four hours including stops, but the clock goes back ten hours during the journey) and the trip from Sydney to Wellington takes a little more time than is occupied by an excellent meal and a cigarette. Internal air services too are admirable. From Melbourne to Bowen, an endless journey by train, can be done via Townsville in eight hours comfortably. For messages the teleprinter gives instant delivery between all works and their head offices in Melbourne or Wellington.

The business of today simply could not be conducted by the surface travel and surface mail of yesterday. Time means so much more. One

wonders what Thomas Borthwick in his silk hat, selling live cattle in Stanley Market, would think of it all.

Statistical Note

Thomas Borthwick & Sons (U.S.A.) Limited was incorporated in 1960 with an issued capital of £25,000. Formed as a new 'umbrella' to take over and expand largely existing business—meat and pelts—its turnover was some £7 million ($19½ million) in 1961–62. Of course, this is only a part of the firm's American business, much of which is done direct between the company in Australia and New Zealand and their American customers.

Palletised cartoned meat

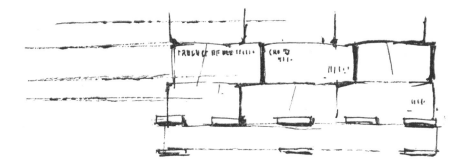

CHAPTER TWELVE

Points of View

Our story has reached its end; or rather it has caught up with the present. Before it is committed to the printer's hands, there remain some things to be said. So far the aim has been to record events. What follows is different. It is extremely relevant and not without interest for many. But it seems only fair to tell the reader, before he embarks on this chapter, that it is mainly concerned with points of view, and that the evidence put forward in support is (necessarily) set out in some detail. If he cannot be bothered with this kind of thing he knows what to do.

Borthwicks sell meat to retail butchers but not directly to the public. A housewife may ask her butcher for 'New Zealand' or 'Australian' lamb but never for 'Borthwicks'; so Borthwicks are quite unlike the owners of a proprietary brand of goods such as Oxo or Bovril who have to try to keep their names before the public. Consequently, the firm has never needed to advertise to the public and such advertisements would have been a waste of time. (They do of course advertise to retail butchers in trade papers.) And until very recently the directors have felt that, theirs being a private company, the way it was run, and the reasons why they thought this was the right way to run it, were their own affair. But during recent years these matters have been attracting more and more public interest. Statements have been made by politicians, in the Press and elsewhere that seemed to call for an answer; and some of the things said were not in accordance with the facts. So Borthwicks felt for the first time the need to explain the facts, and themselves, to the world. They realised then that they had no means of doing so.

Some steps have been taken already, especially in New Zealand. Representatives have been going round talking on these subjects to farmers and anyone who was interested enough to listen. A colour film, 'The Link', was made showing how the wholesale meat trade works in Britain, and this has been and is being shown to farmers and in a number of public cinemas throughout New Zealand. It is hoped that this book—though in fact it is occasioned by the firm's centenary—and this chapter in particular will incidentally help towards the same end.

How the business works

First some remarks about how the meat trade works and the part played in it by competition. It is in general an affair of small units. There are of course some very big farmers and some companies owning chains of retail shops. But these are exceptions, and their size doesn't give them such an advantage that they can put the smaller man out of business. So it does not take great financial resources to set up as a cattle or sheep farmer or a retail butcher.

When we come to the intermediate stages—dealers, exporters, wholesalers—the finance required is rather more but it is still not great. You can be an exporter without owning a freezing works because you can have your stock killed at someone else's works. And even a freezing works does not cost anything like as much to build as, say, a steel rolling mill. Plenty of works have been started by farmers' co-operatives.

The effect of this is that in the meat trade the ordinary, healthy forces of supply and demand really work. If a farmer doesn't like the price one buyer offers for his livestock he can go to another buyer. If he cannot get the price he wants from any buyer he has probably got a false idea of the 'right' price. The price may be lower than usual one year; but, with free competition working all along the line, it is fairly certain that this will be a reflection of economic conditions which no one can help. If the market is being unfairly controlled by some kind of 'get-together', that is another matter: but 'get-togethers' have never lasted long in the meat trade. Borthwicks have in any case, as a matter of principle, always refused to have anything to do with them if they meant agreements on either buying or selling prices. This is dealt with in other parts of the book.

True, the market may sometimes be over-sensitive. Prices may go up or down more than is reasonable in response to prospects of good or bad weather, strikes, revolutions, wars, financial crises, and so on. Here individuals and firms who know their business can do much to cushion the effects of undue optimism or pessimism by taking a longer view.

If anyone thinks that farmers—or dealers or exporters or butchers—are making excessive profits he can, at least with a few supporters, start up in competition himself. And, again, it is a little more difficult but not impossible to start a meat works if you can get some financial backing (and, in New Zealand, a licence)—which is, after all, only what old Thomas Borthwick started doing in 1902 at Waitara.

Further, a farmer can dispose of his stock in various ways—to a local butcher, at an auction, to a drafter representing a freezing works that ships on owner's account, to a drafter working for a farmers' co-operative, or to a buyer representing a firm like Borthwicks. He can choose the way he thinks will give him the best profit. These methods are not all available to all farmers at all places at all times. A dissertation on what happens in different districts and different countries would take too long, but the description is broadly true. In any case, it should be made clear that there is competition not only between different firms but between different methods.

In theory anyway—in practice there may be grave difficulties in many cases—if a farmer thinks that the long-term prospects of stock raising are not good enough he can turn to dairy farming or fruit or crops. In this sense meat production itself is in competition with other kinds of farming. To some extent the same applies to the retail butcher, who can always use his premises for a different business. If the exporters failed to offer both the farmers and the butchers prices good enough to encourage them to carry on, the business of exporters would diminish to a point where equilibrium of supply and demand was reached at a lower level of supplies. The meat trade is one where orthodox marginal economics apply. A lower price in the very long run will result in smaller supplies, and smaller supplies in the long run will mean higher prices. Equilibrium is reached when these two factors, if plotted on a graph as two lines, cut across each other. If the business became unprofitable for the marginal producer, he would in the long run go out of business and the remainder would get a higher price.

Meat production, processing and marketing are carried on by individuals and concerns, some of whom are fairly large but most of them small, all in competition with each other. They have a choice of methods. And their numbers are big enough to ensure that the forces of supply and demand really work, and that anyone who tries to make an excessive profit, or cannot make a reasonable profit at the prices established on a free market, will soon be out of business.

This description of how the meat trade works—as accurate as it can be without being too long or cumbersome—is given because it is the best answer to critics of private enterprise. Whatever may be said of other trades, the meat trade is one—perhaps *the* one above others—in which free competition allows the laws of supply and demand to work. Monopoly is impossible. Governments, the watchdogs of the people's rights, can intervene to check abuses, and to ensure that conditions are favourable to free and honest working. If they try to do more than that, they are interfering with a sensitive mechanism, a living mechanism that has grown up in response to living needs and answers those needs remarkably well. Such interference, except of course in times of national emergency, will probably do more harm than good. The real answer to a critic of the trade is that, if it is as easy as all that, then there is no reason (providing he is a person of moderate substance) why he should not 'have a go' himself. In this respect the meat trade is quite different from, say, oil, where the finance needed is miles out of reach of an individual or even a syndicate.

Some may like a little more detail about how stock is bought and meat sold—the vital points where market forces can be seen at work to establish prices. For them the following two digressions.

Digression on buying

There are two main methods of buying livestock; and this applies to the United Kingdom, Australia and New Zealand. One is what for want of a better name may be called the weight and grade basis, and the other is per head. Due to the wide variation in skin values, sheep and lambs are generally bought per head in Australia, and a big proportion of sheep in New Zealand. The meaning of buying per head is easily understood, whether it be on the farm or in the saleyard. In either case ownership changes on the spot and that is that.

Weight and grade buying (usually called 'schedule buying' in New Zealand) is rather more complicated. It is generally applied to purchases of lambs and ox beef in New Zealand and to cattle buying in parts of Australia. It means in effect that the stock does not change ownership at the farm, but the meat is valued and changes ownership after passing through the works, and is paid for according to its weight and grade. All works in Australia and New Zealand (certainly all Borthwicks' works) charge a killing rate which also covers such items as processing, freezing and loading out, and the works take the offal as a perquisite. In the case of a farmer consigning on his own account the farmer still owns the meat and also the skin (or, if he wants it fellmongered, the wool and pelt).

Killing rates are not the same throughout Australia and New Zealand, but, thanks to competition, neighbouring works must follow each other pretty closely. So far as Borthwicks are concerned it makes no difference for this purpose whether the stock is killed at their own works or at 'outside' works—the rates are the same.

In New Zealand the schedule price offered to the farmer is a quotation per pound for the bare meat 'at works'. In arriving at this figure, account is taken not only of the value of the meat and the skin and the charge for works treatment, but also of all the various costs likely to be incurred between the works and point of sale (in Britain, America, or wherever the major part of that class of meat is sold): these costs include freight, insurance, dock dues, transport, cold storage, bank interest and selling expenses. The schedule, which is of course dictated by competition between operators, will vary according to quality and the weight of the beasts. In the case of a farmer shipping on his own account there will also probably be a drafting fee. There will also in some cases be a debit for transport from the farm to the works. Offals do not come into the picture as they are a works perquisite and therefore part of the treatment rate.

It will be seen that variations in the livestock schedule can be brought about by factors other than a change in the outlook for meat. For instance, if skin values go up the farmer will get more—or the exporter's meat will cost him less; and an increase in freight or works treatment charges will have the opposite effect. An increase in treatment charges can come about for many reasons: a fall in the market value of casings, tallow or offal, or a rise in wages, provided it applies to all works.

The farmer selling on schedule is paid for his meat according to weight and grade as shown on the killing slip, a copy of which is attached to his cheque. Farmers are encouraged to come and see their stock killed, although in fact not many do so.

This description of schedule buying applies to New Zealand. In Australia, cattle buying in Queensland is done on weight and grade basis as in New Zealand with the value of the hide included in the bare meat quotation.

Schedule (or weight and grade) buying, properly conducted, is neither more nor less expensive than per head buying. It is easier to control; but only where conditions are favourable. Any experienced buyer should be able to work on either system. The two have grown up side by side to fit different conditions.

In Britain, until recently, almost all fatstock was sold through the auction ring. The weight of the live beast is recorded on a clock in view of all, and butchers, dealers and the like bid and buy. The auction system can lead to abuse and has not been popular in some farming districts; nevertheless, auctioneers have contributed to the advance of British livestock production by their preparedness to finance the purchase of store cattle and generally to afford generous credit.

A swing to weight and grade buying has been brought about by the inauguration of the Fatstock Marketing Corporation in 1954 and by the changes that this body has imposed upon the whole system of marketing livestock in the United Kingdom. The larger wholesalers and manufacturers, many of whom own slaughterhouses and retail outlets, have encouraged weight and grade purchases. This system also lends itself to a simple application of the Government's Deficiency Payments Scheme.

Digression on selling

Though in Britain all meat is sold per pound, there are once again two different methods of selling. When the butcher buys home-killed meat or imported chilled beef (which can vary in quality from quarter to quarter), he usually likes to see what he is buying and will pay more for a carcase or cut that appeals to him. So most of this meat is sold at market stalls or depots, where butchers go round inspecting, using their judgment in competition one with another, and buying from wholesalers who are also competing with each other to offer the best value.

On the other hand frozen meat from Australia and New Zealand is so efficiently graded that much of it is sold on description without being seen by the buyer. In fact, many orders are put through by telephone. The method is simple and saves a good deal of time. But still the same market forces work. The butcher has to judge what his customers want and how much they will pay, and the wholesaler has to offer what the butchers want at the price the butchers will pay.

The point to be emphasised is that here again two systems have grown up side by side to fit conditions. If either failed to give results satisfactory to the butcher and his customers, and to the farmers whose meat is being sold, it would simply cease. The fact is that in Britain, where the market is free, the consumer gets at least as good value and (equally important where food is concerned) as wide a choice as anywhere in the world.

Profits, taxes and depreciation

We have seen what views were held about profits by Thomas Borthwick, the typical Victorian merchant. When an opportunity came along to enable his firm to earn larger profits he would have considered it a moral weakness to refuse, even though he himself was in no need of money and the change involved him in great personal inconvenience. Ideas have altered a good deal since his day. But profits remain essential. They are not only the great incentive to effort and the reward of success. (This aspect is sometimes exaggerated. Some able men work hard without considering the money for which they have little use.) They are also a test. They prove that a business is answering a public need and that it is being efficiently run.

But there is another vital point to remember when people talk as if the making of profits were in some way a crime. Profits provide for the maintenance, repair and renewal of plant and machinery. They also provide for modernisation and improvement, and for the constant work of research and development without which no firm can keep 'with it' in these times and continue to play its part in the world's economic life. (New developments can of course be financed by other means such as borrowing or issuing additional shares. But Borthwicks have always taken pride in the fact that their business has been built up by ploughing back money that was earned.)

Reference has already been made to taxation and the effect it can sometimes have in putting a brake on development.

What follows is a particular instance. It illustrates some of these points both about the use of profits and about the incidence of taxation. It follows and amplifies something that was said in Chapter Ten about the situation in which Borthwicks found themselves at the end of the second world war and the problem of replacing worn-out assets in a time of inflation.

To show the problem in its simplest terms, let us suppose for a moment that instead of Borthwicks we are dealing with a one-man business whose only asset is a motor lorry. (Even now we shall have to ignore many details and confine ourselves to the essentials.) First, let us go back to a time of fairly stable costs and suppose that our friend buys his lorry in 1925. It might cost him, then, £500. If he is wise he will realise that it will not last for ever and that he will have to scrap it in ten years. So he writes its value down in his books at an annual rate of 10 per cent and saves up £50 every year to buy a new one. This money he puts aside out of his profits; and—this is important—the tax inspector allows him to count the £50 'depreciation' as a business expense and to deduct it from his income for tax purposes. In 1935 his old lorry is ready for the scrap heap: but he has £500 saved up to buy a new one.

Now suppose that he does the same thing in 1950. The value of money has gone down and (the same thing essentially) prices have gone up. Instead of £500 his lorry now costs him £1,000. Provident as ever, he writes it down at 10 per cent; but this time he has to save £100 a year. However, the tax inspector allows him the £100 tax free.

But now prices continue to rise. Half-way through, in 1955, he realises that a new lorry is going to cost him £2,000. He has only saved £500 so far. In the next five years he has got to save £1,500; that is, £300 a year.

That is bad enough. But there is worse to come. The tax inspector sticks to the original valuation based on 'historical cost'. No more allowances. Our poor friend has got to save the additional £200 a year out of *taxed* income. Assuming that he pays tax at 7s. 9d. in the £, he must really save, not £300 a year, but £427 (£100 tax free, £327 subject to £127 tax).

In practice, a man with one lorry would probably merely 'bear in mind' that he had to save enough to get a new one when the old one was worn out, but a bigger business can hardly leave matters with the pious hope that 'it will come all right on the day'. It is necessary to get some idea of what the sum needed to be saved will amount to. (It is also of course necessary to save it!)

This, essentially, was the position which Borthwicks, and indeed all firms with money invested in bricks and mortar and machinery, had to face after the second world war and have been facing ever since. The only important difference was that instead of one lorry they had eight (later nine) freezing works in Australia and New Zealand, besides Borthwick Wharf and the Lancashire Cold Store, all of which had been worked very hard for five years with virtually no maintenance at all.

In addition, improvements were needed to bring the works up to date, and in some cases extensions to cope with increased killings. The advent of the American market also involved great expenditure on new boning rooms.

Money had been set aside out of past earnings to pay for the replacement of worn-out assets, although only enough to pay for it at pre-war prices was allowed tax free. Meanwhile costs had multiplied several times and (what was not foreseen in 1946 but was certainly appreciated a few years later) costs went on rising; this has never seriously looked like ceasing.

This problem of replacing worn-out assets at several times their pre-war costs had of course a bearing on new investments; the directors had to consider carefully before going ahead with any new ventures or they would have been using money that they were going to need to replace existing assets when they wore out. There were plenty of opportunities and plenty of bright ideas. But bright ideas have to be considered in relation to resources available. Since the end of the second world war 'profits' have been at a level that at first sight seems satisfactory; but the persistence of inflation, plus the incidence of taxation, has definitely acted as a brake on further development.

If anyone still has an appetite for facts and figures, here are some more. The way Borthwicks made sure of facing up to the problem of depreciation-plus-inflation was by revaluing their fixed assets. This was exactly what our friend with the lorry might have done—to re-reckon the cost of replacement at current prices and the amount of money that must be set aside yearly to cover depreciation. But for Borthwicks, it was a big operation.

Revaluation had to be done in any case for insurance purposes. It was done in 1954, the year of decontrol.

The effect was to increase the total book value of all the firm's fixed assets by over £5 million. This of course did not mean that the firm was any better off. It simply meant that the purchasing power of money had dropped; and that, if all these assets were suddenly wiped out by an Act of God—like Paki Paki—the cost of replacement would in fact be £5 million more than the old book value. The extra depreciation on this larger sum represented the extra amount that had to be set aside to cover the replacements and renewals that would certainly become necessary—not to increase efficiency but to keep it at its present level. If they didn't do this the whole firm would be gradually running down like an unwound clock. The result for them would be the same as for our friend with the lorry if he failed to save enough to get a new one. They would eventually go out of business.

And—an important point—this extra money that had to be put aside out of earnings was not allowed for tax purposes. It all had to be saved out of taxed profits.

Incidentally the 1954 revaluation was not a permanent solution. The purchasing power of money has continued to drop. Already at the time of writing, 1963, it has become evident that the values of nine years ago are out of date, and that the money being set aside is not enough.

The proper way to face up to the present situation would be another re-valuation. But this would be an enormous task. And it would not make any difference to the tax inspector.

To drive the point home, let us quote the actual figures for one particular Borthwick works. In 1954 the amount set aside for depreciation was £15,030 and the amount allowed for tax £13,100. Not a very big discrepancy. Then came the revaluation. In 1955 the amount set aside for depreciation jumped to £76,103. Of this, £15,500 was allowed for tax.

The totals for this works over the years 1955–61 are: depreciation actually written off, £525,109; allowed for tax, £148,500. In these seven years the firm has had to set aside out of *taxed* earnings £376,609 to keep the works up to date and efficient. This for one works.

So anyone can see that 'profits' are required for other purposes than going into the shareholders' pockets.

Here are some more figures about this particular works, but over a rather longer period, 1951 to 1961, to demonstrate the *cash flow* compared with the capital expenditure. *Cash flow*, by the way, is just what it sounds like: it is the cash earned and available for all purposes—capital expendi-ture, keeping some cash in reserve for later expansion or against a rainy day, contributing to head office expenses, or to paying a dividend. You will note that the company's revaluation of fixed assets mentioned on page 201 comes in the middle of our period, in 1954.

Only one other matter, perhaps, is not obvious. Why is the net profit struck after deducting $2\frac{1}{2}$ per cent interest on the book value of the works? This *prior charge* on the profits before calculating the *cash flow* is proper, be-cause if the works was leased to the person running it, he would have to pay something in rent; or if this person owned the works, it would have *cost* him something either to borrow the money to build it, or (if he had enough money of his own) in lost interest on the money he could have lent to somebody else. This $2\frac{1}{2}$ per cent *prior charge* is to take notice of this rent charge, or interest paid, or interest lost. The only possible quibble is that

$2\frac{1}{2}$ per cent seems a low rate of interest. Bear in mind that if the rate were higher, the *cash flow* would be less.

	Net profit after tax; depreciation allowed for tax; and interest on the value of the works at $2\frac{1}{2}\%$	To arrive at cash flow we must add back depreciation allowed for tax	Cash flow (extra cash available for all purposes)	Compared to capital expenditure as in the accounts	Book value of works in the accounts	Depreciation actually written off in annual accounts based on the book value – compare this with column (2)
	(1)	(2)	(3)	(4)	(5)	(6)
	£000	£000	£000	£000	£000	£000
1951	18	9	27	10	444	11
1952	27	13	40	12	501	15
1953	5	13	18	14	566	15
1954	42	13	55	33	1,062	15
1955	9	15	24	42	1,340	76
1956	15	21	36	54	1,362	78
1957	6	26	32	28	1,337	85
1958	2	24	26	17	1,275	77
1959	8	22	30	29	1,257	72
1960	37	20	57	44	1,191	69
1961	27	21	48	57	1,163	68
	196	197	393	340		581

Why a private company?

Will Borthwicks become a public company? The directors had hardly discussed this question among themselves: they were unanimously determined to remain a private company and that was that. But with this book in view they thought it worth while, as an interesting exercise, to consider their reasons.

To begin with, is there any inducement to change? If Borthwicks became a public company, or if they sold out to a competitor, the result would be to increase the shareholders' bank balances by exchanging share certificates with a face value of £1 for cash considerably in excess. On the other hand, there would be certain difficulties in a straightforward sale to the public. The imported meat business is highly speculative. It has some very good years and some very bad ones. The present shareholders (members of one family with ample means outside the business and therefore independent of dividends) are used to this sort of thing and take it in their stride. So long as, on balance, the profits are more than the losses, and so long as the margin is enough to keep the business going, it is all right with them. But such variations are not popular with merchant banks and other institutions who specialise in floating new concerns, nor with most private investors.

A competitor might make an offer; but there are reasons why it is not particularly likely. The meat trade, as has been said, is largely an affair of small units. This is because there are no great advantages, in the way of streamlining and reduced overhead costs, to be had from very large-scale organisation. It is doubtful whether anyone would gain much from a merger.

So Borthwicks might not be a particularly easy company to sell, at any rate at the price which its present owners think it is worth.

In any case they don't want to sell it. After some self-examination the directors concluded that their first reason is what the chairman describes as 'emotional'. The business represents a considerable achievement in which they take some pride. (The directors of the parent company, re-member, are all descendents of Thomas Borthwick except the four executive directors, two of whom started with the firm as office boys.)

Their second reason is frankly selfish and yet difficult to disentangle from the first. They and various junior members of the family have got interesting jobs in the firm which they would be sorry to lose, because they enjoy them.

The third reason, which again is almost impossible to separate from the others, might be described as emotional, selfish or unselfish as you choose. It is linked with the outlook of Thomas Borthwick, who felt bound to carry on and expand the business without considering his own convenience and although he didn't want any more money. He would probably have called it a moral duty if he had been compelled to explain himself. The present directors would express themselves differently but their feelings are no doubt much the same. In any case they want to carry on the work that their grandfather started. This is not primarily a matter of making profits. It is the satisfaction that comes from doing a job properly.

Ever since the business started Borthwicks have felt that their mission in life was to bridge, as efficiently as possible, the gap between the farmer in Australia and New Zealand and the British butcher. They consider that up to now the job has been done reasonably successfully, and they believe that, if it had not been for Borthwicks, the farmer would have received rather less for his stock, or else the butcher would have had to pay a little more for his meat, or both. They feel pretty sure that this job has been done more effectively than it could have been if Borthwicks had been a public company. This view they explain as follows.

A public company is under a much more definite obligation to make money for its shareholders than is a private company, particularly if the private company's shareholders are all sufficiently well off to be independent of dividends. This has some interesting consequences. In the meat business with its ups and downs, its shocks and opportunities, senior men are continually making decisions requiring freedom of action, nerve and confidence. They need to know that they are going to be backed up when they make mistakes. If you watch Borthwicks at work anywhere in Britain, Australia or New Zealand, one of the first things you notice is that people are not afraid to make decisions. They do so as a matter of course. It seems to come naturally. The feeling filters down from the top. But in a highly speculative business some decisions will obviously turn out to be wrong and there might be a reluctance to make decisions if people were liable to be flung out by angry shareholders. This has a bearing on the psychology of the people actually at the top of the business. Borthwicks have always been careful to trade well within the limits of their resources, but that could not prevent, in a highly speculative business, a big swing from gains to losses and back again. It will be common knowledge to any readers of this book who are card players that a person is unlikely to play a good game of bridge if he cannot afford to pay when he loses. To continue the family metaphor, it can be added that a person would be unlikely to make the best of his hand, even if he could afford to pay, if he was afraid he was going to get into trouble with his wife afterwards. (In this context for 'wife' read 'shareholders'.)

To pay the farmer a little more than the absolute minimum price prevailing in bad times, or to sell meat at less than the maximum to try and get a new market started in some part of the world, means cutting profit margins. In other words (remembering the many uses to which profits have to be put) it may mean that the chances of a respectable dividend will be less. To put up with this is not pure unselfishness. It is a matter of taking a long view and of playing one's part in keeping the whole industry on an even keel in a storm. The Borthwick family have always understood this and taken the rough weather with the smooth. The shareholders of a public company might well take a different view. Knowing little about the business except that they were getting nothing out of it at the moment, they might well conclude that there was inefficiency somewhere and call for someone's blood. Again, after a particularly good year they might well claim more than their due. (When considering this argument, it must be remembered that there is no comparable public company whose ordinary shares are quoted on the London Stock Exchange.)

There is a further point which, although it hardly ever arises, is of some interest. On the whole, the making of money is a sign that a show is properly run, but a concern that is not acting as a trustee for the shareholders in the sense that the directors of a public company usually are, can sometimes take a line as a matter of principle even although such a line is unlikely to make money. Reference has been made on page 131 to Borthwicks' refusal to enter a 'get together'. In the very short run they could have made more money by agreeing to this. In the light of later events, and particularly of the large profits they made in the several years subsequent to it, it looks as though the decision cost them nothing and may well have gained them something; but the point is that a public company would be more likely to have felt impelled to join in, whereas Borthwicks were able to indulge in the luxury of staying outside even though at the time it appeared less profitable. Whether this was right or wrong or good or bad is not here in question. The point is that Borthwicks were able, as a private company, to take a line on grounds other than mere profit making.

Here a brief explanation of a point which has been the subject of some public misunderstanding. Borthwicks are an 'exempt' private company. This means simply that they are exempt from certain provisions of the United Kingdom Companies Act which require that proper accounts be filed with the Registrar. To qualify for exemption a company must fulfil certain conditions, one of which is that it must have less than fifty shareholders. Company law aims to protect shareholders from the machinations of directors and executives: but if the shareholders are only a few, particularly of one family, they are deemed to be able to look after themselves.

There is no particular advantage in exemption, except that it saves a little trouble, and perhaps some people prefer that their incomes should not be exposed to the public and the Press. Borthwicks are a large company as private companies go (they are probably among the first twenty exempt private companies in the United Kingdom). But this needs to be seen in proper perspective. If they were a public company with issued capital of £1,650,000 plus some revenue reserves they would only be rated as a medium-sized one. They therefore do not flatter themselves that the world is waiting to pounce on their accounts.

The recent Jenkins Report recommended that this exemption should cease and that all private companies should be required to file accounts. So it looks as if the question may be of no more than academic interest in a year or two. So far as Borthwicks are concerned it will not make any difference.

Could anything compel or induce Borthwicks to change their minds and become a public company? This might have happened long ago if fortune had not presented Thomas Borthwick with four sons. It might have happened later if one of those sons had had a family consisting entirely of girls. And here the shadow of the tax inspector falls on the page once more. Suppose this had occurred, and suppose these girls had married men with businesses of their own. On their father's death his shares in the firm would go to them. They might well have decided to convert these shares into cash to invest in their husbands' businesses. Borthwicks, like most private companies, have a clause in their articles that any shareholder wishing to sell shares must offer them first to an existing shareholder: and it has been laid down that a private company cannot stipulate a price; the price must be 'reasonable'. The existing shareholders would naturally want to buy these shares, but could they have found the money? They were reasonably well off, but if two or three offers of this sort were made it might have been beyond them. It is almost certain that in this event Borthwicks would have become a public company or sold out to a competitor.

The same situation could arise in the future but it is extremely unlikely. Four of Thomas Borthwick's grandsons are full-time directors of the company today; there are three great-grandsons in the business or about to come in, and several males of the next generation already in existence. Moreover, as time goes on the shares become wider spread.

Probably the commonest cause that compels a private company to become public is a demand for death duties. If the money to meet this demand cannot be found by other means, shares have to be sold, and the company becomes public to get a quotation. Fortunately this is unlikely to happen to Borthwicks. The family are modest spenders. (Is this something to do with Presbyterian ancestry?) The shares are spread over a respectable number of Thomas Borthwick's grandchildren and great-grandchildren, who between them have saved enough to meet any demand for death duties that can be foreseen at present. What the situation would be should the British Exchequer become even more voracious than it is now, no one can say.

Of course, it is always conceivable that the directors might lose interest in the business and decide to sell it if a good offer came along. The feelings expressed elsewhere in this chapter are based on realities and evidently go deep. They could only change—and then there would have to be some painful tearing up of roots—if something were to change those realities: if the conditions that make the meat industry what it is—the feeling that there is a real job to be done, risks to be taken, opportunities to be grasped, storms to be ridden, room for judgment and initiative—were destroyed. Suppose, for instance, that in a wide extension of Government control some form of price control was clamped down on all sources of supply at each stage. If something on these lines happened the interest would disappear and there would be a call for an 'agonising re-appraisal'.

There is plenty of room for change. The meat business would not be what it is if things did not change constantly and often unpredictably. Our story is a story of change. In this one respect—the character and constitution of Borthwicks—we are entitled to hope that there will be no change.

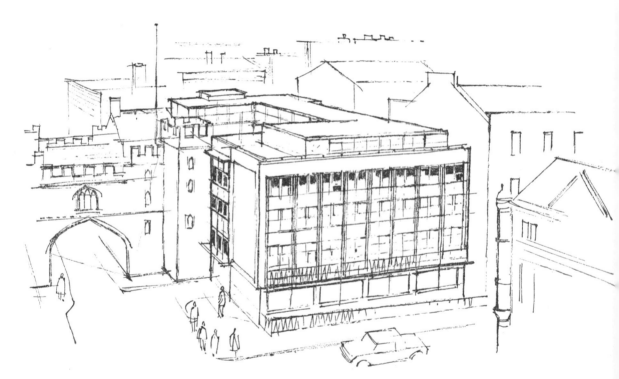

Priory House, St John's Lane, London

Senior Staff Appointments in Australia and New Zealand

As so few have been mentioned by name in the text, the Australian and New Zealand managements have asked for some of their senior men to be recorded in an appendix. Whom to choose was a fairly simple question as in both countries there were a number of quite big and separate 'commands'. But this is not so in Britain where the business consists of a large number of relatively small units: the list would be so long and where to draw the line so difficult that it is perhaps prudent not to begin to try.

Australian Executives

GENERAL MANAGER
19..–10 N. W. Kingdon
1910–11 J. Whittingham
1911–45 J. S. Balderstone, Snr.
1945–53 G. B. Robertson
1953–   J. S. Balderstone, Jnr.

ASSISTANT GENERAL MANAGER
1938–41 S. F. Olliff
1953–62 W. E. Shimmin
1962–   D. S. A. McFarlane

ADMINISTRATIVE MANAGER
1953–   P. F. J. Kendall

WORKS SUPERINTENDENT
1927–45 G. B. Robertson
1948–51 J. Simpson
1957–   K. R. Ross

LIVESTOCK MANAGER
1946–   H. E. Nolte

SALES MANAGER
1950–60 S. Simpson
1960–   C. J. Cole

MANAGER—EXPORT DEPARTMENT
1950–   F. C. Boniface

BY-PRODUCTS SALES MANAGER
1945–   J. C. Gillies

SECRETARY
19..–37 H. B. Griffiths
1937–41 A. P. Hamilton
1941–50 A. C. Beckett
1950–54 K. Smith
1954–60 C. J. Cole
1960–62 N. J. Spalding
1962–   M. J. Plumbridge

SHIPPING MANAGER
1954–   L. W. Thomas

PASTORAL INSPECTOR
1948–62 H. K. Goodwin
1962–   T. M. Borthwick

Bowen Branch and Works
MANAGER
1896–1934 Mr Marshall
1934–54 E. W. Saker

BRANCH MANAGER
1958–   G. A. G. Dear

WORKS MANAGER
1954–58 G. A. G. Dear
1958–   G. F. Orford

Brisbane Branch—Moreton Works
BRANCH MANAGER
1912–15 George Sproat
1915–36 Gilbert Lees
1936–42 R. G. A. Dear
1942–62 A. A. Van Homrigh

WORKS MANAGER
1912–19 C. V. Parkinson

1919–34 M. L. Moss
1936–48 J. Simpson
1948–51 A. E. Wing
1951–60 J. Simpson
1960–   D. Main

Melbourne Branch—Brooklyn Works
MANAGER
1909–10 Mr Duncan
1910–11 C. V. Parkinson
1912–13 Mr Eggleston
1913–14 A. H. Leeson
1914–30 G. W. Boulton
1930–36 J. Simpson
1936–48 D. MacLeod

BRANCH MANAGER
1948–62 W. King
1962–   N. J. Spalding

WORKS MANAGER
1948–58 D. MacLeod
1959–   N. J. McLennan

Portland Branch and Works
MANAGER
1905–12 A. H. L. Barton
1913–20 A. H. Leeson
1921–29 C. V. Parkinson
1929–60 H. Keiller

BRANCH MANAGER
1960–62 W. S. Norton
1962–   N. C. Myers

WORKS MANAGER
1960–   K. A. McDonald

Yahl Works
WORKS MANAGER
1948–49 F. W. Pengelly
1949–54 C. J. Woosley
1954–59 W. S. Norton
1959–61 T. M. Borthwick
1961–   J. H. Monger

Albany Branch and Works

MANAGER
1948–   W. J. L. Anderson

LIVESTOCK MANAGER
1948–58 D. S. A. McFarlane

Adelaide Branch

BRANCH MANAGER
1935–46 H. E. Nolte
1947–49 O. Cruse

1949–56 G. Garrick
1956–62 N. C. Myers
1962–   P. M. J. Crowe

Sydney Branch

BRANCH MANAGER
1921–44 J. E. D. Bryce
1947–54 L. W. Thomas
1954–55 C. Milson
1955–57 W. G. Patrick
1960–   J. A. Sealey

New Zealand Executives

GENERAL MANAGER
1910–21 C. S. Harper
1921–30 W. H. E. Flint
1930–56 E. G. Norman
1956–59 M. H. R. Sandwith
1959–   P. T. Norman

ASSISTANT GENERAL MANAGER
1962–   W. R. Mathieson

STOCK MANAGER
1930–61 A. Corskie
1962–   G. P. Stapleton

ADMINISTRATIVE MANAGER
1955–61 W. R. Mathieson
1961–   H. J. Hayes

SECRETARY FOR NEW ZEALAND
1903–30 C. H. White (Accountant)
1930–31 A. E. Cree
1931–44 E. R. Rogers
1944–54 W. R. Mathieson
1955–61 H. J. Hayes
1961–   C. M. G. Herriot

SHIPPING MANAGER
1928–42 A. W. Charleson
1942–   G. Chambers

SALES MANAGER
1946–   A. L. Paterson

WORKS SUPERINTENDENT
1946–56 T. C. H. Miller
1956–   D. Freeman

SUPERINTENDENT ENGINEER
1915–34 G. R. Croll
1934–46 W. G. Baird
1947–   E. Blacker

BY-PRODUCTS MANAGER
1960–   F. M. Ollivier

SOUTH ISLAND MANAGER
1930–49 A. C. Wells
1949–56 A. I. Guild
1956–   T. C. H. Miller

District Managers

NORTHLAND
1946–   E. L. Brodie

TARANAKI
1946–54 P. J. Allen
1954–   N. G. Vickers

WAIRARAPA
1952–53 P. T. Norman
1954–59 S. G. Stewart
1959–   A. W. Lawrence

MANAWATU
1946–59 B. H. Pringle
1960–   J. King

TOKOMARU BAY
1946–52 N. G. Vickers

WAIKATO
1940–49 F. H. Anderson

HAWKES BAY
1946–53 C. D. Taaffe
1953–   W. B. Farquharson

CANTERBURY
1954–60 G. P. Stapleton
1960–   A. Watson

INVERGARGILL
1931–53 R. H. Lawrence

District Representatives
INVERCARGILL
1960–62 A. I. Smith
1962–   W. Sligh

Manawatu Meat & Cold Storage Co. Ltd
1946–47 L. Bartlett
1947–53 W. E. Shimmin
1953–54 P. T. Norman
1954–   J. Sampson

Works Managers
CANTERBURY
1916–20 L. Smaill
1920–31 W. G. Baird

1931–38 F. S. Smaill
1938–40 J. W. Weir
1940–46 O. A. Keith
1946–48 J. W. Weir
1949–56 A. Heath
1956–   C. H. Croucher

WAITARA
1903–05 W. L. Gray
1905–15 G. R. Croll
1915–17 A. R. Lennon
1917–46 P. J. Allen
1946–   R. H. Hutchinson

WAINGAWA
1928–31 W. H. Maitland
1931–38 W. G. Baird
1938–51 F. S. Smaill
1951–54 J. King
1954–   G. V. Greer

FEILDING
1931–44 V. J. Stitchbury
1944–50 H. S. Tate
1951–54 G. V. Greer
1954–58 J. King
1959–   D. Constance

PAKI PAKI
1910–26 W. H. Maitland
1926–31 W. L. Wright

TOKOMARU BAY
1944–49 F. E. Porter
1949–52 G. S. P. Chalmers

ALEXANDRA
1939–47 R. Burt
1947–51 F. G. Stanley
1951–53 J. Watson

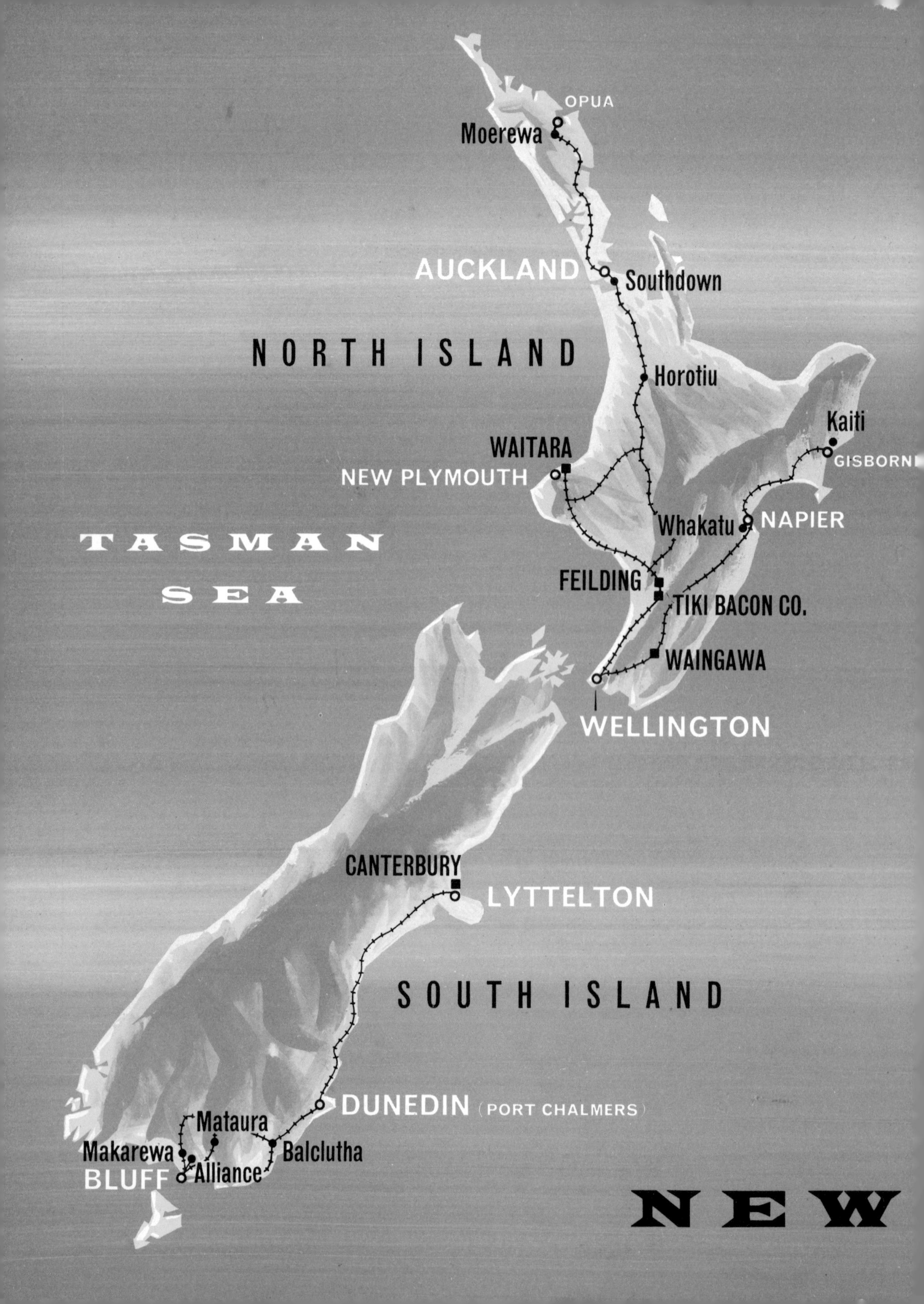

OPUA

Moerewa

AUCKLAND

Southdown

NORTH ISLAND

Horotiu

Kaiti

GISBORN

WAITARA

NEW PLYMOUTH

Whakatu

NAPIER

TASMAN

SEA

FEILDING

TIKI BACON CO.

WAINGAWA

WELLINGTON

CANTERBURY

LYTTELTON

SOUTH ISLAND

DUNEDIN (PORT CHALMERS)

Mataura

Makarewa

Balclutha

BLUFF

Alliance

NEW